THE PURSUIT OF THE
PERSONAL
RENAISSANCE
EXPERIENCE

THE PURSUIT OF THE
PERSONAL RENAISSANCE EXPERIENCE

FINDING OPPORTUNITIES FOR HAPPINESS IN THE EVER-PRESENT NOW

REVISED EDITION 2019

PETER G. JUSTUS, M.D.

ReadersMagnet, LLC

The Pursuit of the Personal Renaissance Experience—Finding Opportunities for Happiness in the Ever-Present Now: Revised Edition 2019
Copyright © 2019 by Peter G. Justus, M.D.

Published in the United States of America
ISBN Paperback: 978-1-950947-03-4
ISBN Hardback: 978-1-950947-12-6
ISBN eBook: 978-1-950947-04-1

All rights reserved. No part of this publication may be reproduced, stored in a retrieval system or transmitted in any way by any means, electronic, mechanical, photocopy, recording or otherwise without the prior permission of the author except as provided by USA copyright law.

The opinions expressed by the author are not necessarily those of ReadersMagnet, LLC.

ReadersMagnet, LLC
10620 Treena Street, Suite 230 | San Diego, California, 92131 USA
1.619. 354. 2643 | www.readersmagnet.com

Book design copyright © 2019 by ReadersMagnet, LLC. All rights reserved.
Cover design by Ericka Walker
Interior design by Shemaryl Evans

CONTENTS

Acknowledgements 7
Foreword 9

Chapter 1: Introduction 11
Chapter 2: Consciousness 12
Chapter 3: My recognition of the Opportunities
 for Happiness in the Ever-Present Now 21
Chapter 4: My Deeper Look at the Sonicare
 Experience—the Realization of the
 Phenomenon of the Personal
 Renaissance Experience 31
Chapter 5: Examination of My Daily Roles 39
Chapter 6: Lessons from Golf 42
Chapter 7: The Biologic Imperatives 50
Chapter 8: The Evolution of Biologic
 and Social Organisms 62
Chapter 9: Application to Other Life Roles 75

Chapter 10: Looking for Process Improvement Opportunities at Work and "Why Do We Allow Ourselves to Suffer at Work and What Can We Do About It?" 78

Chapter 11: Money and Possessions 94

Chapter 12: Citizenship and Morality 99

Chapter 13: The Inevitability of Inter-Group Conflict 103

Chapter 14: Spirituality, Happiness, and Personal Process Improvement 108

Chapter 15: Summary 118

ACKNOWLEDGEMENTS

This book, including its first and now revised edition, would not have been possible without the help of many people. The list begins with my parents, George and Madeleine Justus who survived the horrors of Nazi domination of eastern Europe as well as post-war Soviet occupation and immigrated to the United States in time for me to grow up a member of our baby boomer generation. With their love and gentle encouragement, I gained the confidence it takes to pursue the long course of education and training required to become a physician. I should acknowledge the late Dr. Bertold Bruell, my childhood family doctor in Federal Way, Washington State, whose grace and compassion made him the perfect role model for any young, aspiring medical practitioner. I would like to thank all of my partners in Puget Sound Gastroenterology, particularly my office mate, Dr. Ronald Mason, who, on a daily basis, help me become the best GI doctor I can be.

"The Pursuit of the Personal Renaissance Experience" would not have gotten off the ground without the editorial assistance of my oldest and closest friend dating back to elementary school days, David Campbell. David is the smartest and most talented person I have personally known and his insights were invaluable. His only fault, (although, strictly speaking, "fault" is a contradiction in terms), is his unconditional love for me and practically everyone else close to him.

Lastly, I am most pleased to acknowledge the love and support from my wife of 44 years, Sheila Teama Clevenger Justus. I can't tell you how many times she has saved me from myself. I am truly grateful for her careful reading of the manuscript and helpful suggestions. Also, without her patience with the large number of mental absences it took me to formulate the stream of thoughts required to write a book, neither of us would have been able to survive the process.

FOREWORD

A few years ago, I had an experience that involved a rather mundane, everyday human activity that changed the way I view and live my life. It made me realize how much of my life was spent living through precious, present time rather than living in it. Through this experience and from my perspective as a physician and former student of biology, I developed an understanding of the purpose of human existence which led me to a personal philosophy which helps me live a much more fulfilling life. If you continue on this journey with me, you will be guided through a couple of billion years of evolution, one book on a Viennese school of psychotherapy, several Hollywood movies, a description of the evil gods of golf, a biblical passage or two, an old episode of "Star Trek", and a current Netflix reality show. The initial goal of writing this book was to communicate what I think is very important information to my children. Now I believe that it contains truths that could benefit anyone.

CHAPTER 1

INTRODUCTION

Almost everyone *wants* to be happy. Thomas Jefferson, one of the founding fathers of our country, asserted in the Declaration of Independence that, along with life and liberty, we all ought to have the right to pursue this elusive thing we call happiness. But what is it? When people are asked what they want from life, they will usually opt for "happiness" over wealth, fame, and so on, recognizing that happiness does not result from the mere possession of money or recognition. However, when asked to define what it is that makes them happy, they have a difficult time providing a satisfactory answer.

Over the years, many philosophers, psychologists, and laypersons have expressed their opinions on this issue. In what follows, I will express mine.

CHAPTER 2

CONSCIOUSNESS

The very fact that we human beings can consider an analysis of issues such as the origin of happiness is a testament to our highly developed level of *consciousness*. Our consciousness has allowed us to examine our surroundings, draw conclusions, and, most importantly for us, based on the results of this evaluation, consider potential courses of action that might be beneficial to us. Something within us drives the hope that in the gathering of information there will be *improvements in the understanding of our world*, and in the execution of the indicated actions, there will be an *improvement in some relevant process* over which we can, at least to some degree, exert control. It is hoped that the outcome will be better in a way that, in turn, will somehow make us more successful in our world. Certainly, human consciousness is a profoundly powerful tool that, along with other physical developments (a high degree of manual dexterity, for example), has helped human beings to become the most efficient exploiters of the world's resources.

Compared to other species, we are not the biggest, fastest, or even perhaps the most handsome or graceful group. However, when it comes to the capabilities of the soft, living tissue that occupies that hollow, boney object that sits upon our shoulders, we are the best. One only has to look at the remarkable complexity of our inventions and the effects they have had on our ability to prosper on this planet to see the truth of this. The ultimate proof of this really lies in the steadily rising population of our species (despite wars and epidemics), which currently is over seven and a half billion members worldwide.

I believe that we humans are rewarded for the use of this tool, which, of course, is part of our brain, by feelings of self-fulfillment that are triggered when this tool is employed in a certain way. Stated slightly differently, my assumption is that happiness is a human experience that is strongly related to processes that are directly tied to environmental awareness and exploitation. I will discuss what I believe to be the value of this association later on in this chapter.

When I use a term like "environmental exploitation," I understand that some look at "exploitation" as a negative or evil type of action, such as when one takes advantage of another. (And, in reality, this could be an intended or unintended consequence of any exploitative activity.) What I am specifically talking about is what we all do as individuals or as members of groups to maximize the possibility of our continued existence and ultimately to reproduce ourselves. For example, by breathing, we exploit our environment's supply of oxygen without which we could not survive for more than five or ten minutes. We all need to exploit the environment for sources of energy that keep our bodies intact and functioning and without which we would cease to exist. Of course, people will have different views of whether a certain form of exploitation is bad or good. Examples of this are disagreements over cutting down trees, digging coal out of the ground, the price of gasoline, etc. I believe these judgments play a significant role in the generation of social conflict. I will discuss that in more detail later in another chapter.

Parenthetically, I have to say that although while an advanced level of consciousness is an important factor leading to our biologic success as members of our species, *Homo sapiens*, I don't believe that we are the only multicellular organisms who utilize it. Years ago, I was taught that humans were the only living beings who possess *consciousness* and that the actions of animals are predicated by their "pre-programmed," species-specific, *instincts*. However, we do have evidence of the use of tools by other primates and recognize social behaviors in many animals that suggest at least some level of environmental awareness and rudimentary levels of technological and social adaptation. For example, as revealed a few years ago in a PBS episode of "Nature", crows have been observed to drop whole nuts at a certain height onto concrete roads in order to crack their shells without losing their contents. They time this activity to coincide with red traffic lights to avoid being run over by cars. Could such specific behavior be directly "programmed" by a special arrangement of atoms in their DNA? (There will be more on DNA later!) I do not think so. We, who constitute the species *Homo sapiens*, appear to have the most evolved level of consciousness on earth. It would seem likely that other, now extinct hominids (e.g., *Homo erectus*, *Homo neanderthalensis*) possessed species-specific iterations of consciousness that were less environmentally adaptive than that of *Homo sapiens*. There will be more on this in a later chapter as well. This could then have been a factor in the events that led to their disappearances from the world stage.

"Consciousness" can then be viewed as a tool possessed by different animal species that works in concert with the rest of the central nervous system and its information-gathering extensions—the eyes, ears, nose, taste buds, and peripheral sensory nerves and all the other systems of the body: the musculoskeletal system, the circulatory system, the digestive system, endocrine system, the reproductive system, as well as the outer protective system comprised of the skin. Certainly, the general functional capabilities of any bodily system have a direct bearing on the survival of the individual members of any species under consideration. And therefore, closer to home, the overall biologic success of any human being results from the specific capabilities of all these "tools" and the ways in which they are employed.

I believe that the purpose of these tools is to enhance the survival and therefore the reproductive potential of the individual employing them. I also believe that when we employ them for this purpose, a positive sensation is evoked that reinforces their employment. This could include any activity related to the acquisition of knowledge or material resources, as well as those activities involving interactions with the other human beings who share these goals with us. I believe that we will find "happiness" among these "positive reinforcing sensations".

I must divulge at this point that I have already made a decision, as you will see later, that happiness can be best derived from activities that are *positively-transformative* in a personal way. This bias is reflected in the next few paragraphs in which I assign these potential happiness-engendering experiences to a position on a spectrum.

Beginning at one end of this spectrum, (this is where I am giving myself permission to make a value judgment), it is undeniable that a bowel movement generally leads to a real feeling of satisfaction. Just ask anyone who hasn't had one in a while! The same could be said for emptying a really full urinary bladder. (If you don't believe this, go watch the urinal scene in which the character played by Tom Hanks is introduced to the rest of the baseball team in the movie *A League of Their Own*.) However, I would venture to guess that most people who are truly pursuing deep happiness in their lives are generally not going to feel deeply satisfied in a more global sense by waiting for opportunities to empty their bowels or bladders. Or at least they would not be as likely as I to mention the subject, given what I hear and talk about on a daily basis as a Gastroenterology specialist!

Beyond that, there are other sensory experiences that are associated with other basic physiologic processes which have been appreciated as being highly desirable for people who avidly pursue them. One of these is eating. The pleasure of tasting food and feeling pleasantly full after a meal is understood by virtually everyone. This positive feeling supports the overall function of *energy acquisition*, which is essential to sustaining life. This pleasure is avidly sought all over the world. Just look at the restaurant business. The negative side of this, seen especially in the developed world, is the increasing problem of obesity.

Then there is sex. This driver of the activity, which supports reproduction, is incredibly powerful. Presuming that you can get an honest answer, just ask any fourteen-year-old boy what he thinks the most about during the course of a day. With just a brief look at advertisements in magazines, on television, or the internet, one can see that sex can sell virtually anything. It is, after all, the featured product of the world's oldest profession. There are a few individuals who make sexual intercourse or some of its derivative activities the prime goal of their lives. Just about any kind of orgasm feels good, right? The extreme pleasurable sensations engendered by sexual activity are directly related to the promotion of reproduction, which fulfills life's basic *biologic* purpose—the generation of another life form similar to those who took part in the process.

One of the problems facing the individuals who seeks happiness in their lives with a prime focus on eating or sex, is that the pleasurable sensations last relatively short periods of time and therefore need to be repetitively sought for the individual to stay happy over longer periods of time. This, in turn, often leads to several personal health issues (physical and psychological), as well as societal problems. Overeating leads to obesity with its attendant problems of self-loathing, arthritis, diabetes, hypertension, heart disease, and stroke. Over indulgence in sex can result in unwanted pregnancies, sexually transmitted diseases, as well as in divorce and the associated trauma for all members of the families involved. But even if these are avoided, the practice of a biologic activity divorced from its basic purpose does not have the same intrinsic meaning as when it is carried out directly for that purpose, (e.g., survival and, ultimately, *successful* reproduction). For example, eating when you are really hungry engenders much more satisfaction that when you are full. Sex with a person to whom you have made a deep, lasting commitment evokes a level of deeper, more lasting sense of pleasure than a one-night stand or a masturbation episode. In other words, as eating or sex becomes less connected to its true biologic purpose, it becomes a form of *indulgence.* Don't get me wrong. I, like you, I presume, engage in indulgences and do not, in most instances, feel bad about that fact. Experienced in the right contexts and quantities, an indulgence can be a pleasure, without any harm. Excesses in *quantity* take valuable time away from other, more fulfilling activities. Experiences in a wrong context (e.g., adulterous sex) can, as mentioned above, ruin other relationships that have the potential to render deeper, more enduring meaning.

What about the other end of my spectrum of human activity? Most people would consider religious devotion, non-sexual love, and self-sacrifice for the benefit of family or community to be examples of endeavors leading to a higher order of personal satisfaction. Some (myself included) would put the attainment of a pure spiritual union with God at the pinnacle of such a hierarchy of personal fulfillment. I would distinguish this realm of potential human endeavor as attempts to achieve spiritual immortality and all activities related to survival and reproduction as *de facto* attempts to achieve biologic immortality.

I believe that living in the pursuit of both of these broad goals is important. No one could survive in a physical sense without acting in the realm of the pursuit of biologic immortality to at least some degree. Constant communion with the Almighty would not meet our vital biologic needs. On the other hand, as mentioned above, lust and gluttony may elicit relatively short bursts of highly pleasurable sensations, but in extremes, can be harmful to the health of the individual and also may interfere with the attainment of other more important personal and societal goals.

In summary, a complex but thoughtful approach to living our lives is essential. I believe experiences that involve just the activation of a pleasant sensation evoke more transient, less-enduring feelings of fulfillment than those that involve more complex human functions. My belief is that true happiness is generated by conscious activities that are conceived and executed by the individual. These activities, under certain circumstances, can produce the *positive personal transformation* within an individual to which I referred earlier. Conversely, non-personally transformative experiences like the ones that depend solely on the stimulation of pleasant sensory responses do not generate true, more profound "happiness."

A few years ago, I made an observation that lead me to this conclusion and changed the way I live my life. This occurred after my three children were out of the house (although not all quite "off the payroll," as my wife and I put it) and were either working or were in the final stages of their education. That is, my observation occurred at a time when the most fundamental reason for my daily activities (supporting the functions and success of the family) was not quite so obvious anymore. This observation gave me insight into how one could use time (which, as I get older, is becoming increasingly dear to me) in the most fulfilling ways.

My analysis of this experience led me to believe that we can understand happiness better if we understand what we are all programmed to do by nature. This discussion assumes a willingness to talk about biologic and sociologic evolution (which, I think, are remarkably similar). So, if you believe the currently existing natural world here on Earth was created by an extraterrestrial force in seven consecutive, twenty-four-hour periods and are not open to other opinions, please stop reading this now. It will be a waste of your time. I will say, however, that after many years of seeing many scientific theories rise, fall, and rise again in different forms, it is remotely possible that you are right. I just do not think so. I am very open to the idea that an outside force set all this in motion and, in fact, this is a critical part of the foundation of my faith in God. I also believe that to achieve happiness in the long run, sooner or later we will need the experience of a spiritual presence—a spiritual presence that leads us to truly believe that a part of us is eternal and that the conditions of our *physical* beings are ultimately not that important. Many, "successful" people reach points in their lives where they possess ready access to food, shelter, and all the sensory-stimulating activity that mankind has created, yet they feel desperately lonely despite being surrounded by well-meaning and loving family members and friends. The suicides of celebrities are constant reminders of this phenomenon.

However, for most of this discussion, you do not have to have a belief in any kind of deity or be a member of any specific religious group. Although, you may decide to reconsider this position at some point in the future.

I believe that for most of our lives, personal happiness is derived from a sense that a given unit of time has been spent affecting a *personal* change that results in moving that individual closer toward a desired goal. The scale of the change can be great or small. It does not necessarily matter if others agree that the goal is desirable. It is not essential that the change, initially at least, can be shown to be an improvement by any objective analysis.

In the next few chapters, I will describe an experience I had that led me to this conclusion.

CHAPTER 3

MY RECOGNITION OF THE OPPORTUNITIES FOR HAPPINESS IN THE EVER-PRESENT NOW

I, like many people in our culture, have made regular visits to a dentist ever since childhood. I remember having a fear of the dentist's office when I was young, but I was quite lucky to avoid treatments for cavities until I could handle dental procedure anxiety better as a teenager. Even then, I thought that I did well compared to other kids my age. By high school, I had required only one filling! I can remember eating lunch at the school cafeteria and watching my friends chewing their sandwiches while talking at the same time. This gave me a great opportunity to gain an appreciation of their dental histories. I was clearly struck with the number of teeth surfaces that were embedded with silvery material. I took a great deal of pride in the fact that I would regularly go to the dentist for a checkup and would almost always waltz out with a clean bill of dental health and a quick cleaning job. I considered myself to be the possessor of rather "strong, healthy teeth and gums", a line from one of the toothpaste commercials of the time.

Unfortunately, by the age of thirty-five, things were beginning to change. Okay, time was catching up with me. I had had wisdom teeth extractions and had developed just a few cavities that required fillings and crowns. I considered these events the unfortunate results of the neglect of personal health associated with early adulthood.

However, it was also becoming apparent that I had a dental issue that was about to destroy my formerly held notion of my dental superiority.

My problem was excessive plaque formation. At that time, my family (by then, a total population of five) used the services of a dental office that had been recommended by a family friend who worked there as a dental hygienist. Because of the time required to clean my teeth, that is, to remove the tartar or "calculus" problem that plaque becomes, I was told to come in more and more frequently for cleaning. At one point, rather than a standard six-month interval, I began having to be seen on a three-month schedule and, even then, used up most of the one-hour appointment time. Worse yet, in order to finish on time, even with the frequent visits, they often had to use the dreaded *ultrasonic cleaner*. For me, having an ultrasonic cleaner passed over my teeth was a bit like the proverbial "scratching a fingernail on the blackboard" for twenty minutes straight.

Never-the-less, since this all seemed to evolve over a relatively long period of time, I came to subconsciously accept the situation, and ultimately, despite the ultrasonic cleaning device, actually grew to enjoy my visits for social reasons.

One of the benefits of this extra experience was that I became a master of maintaining the muted side of the dialogue between a dental hygienist and her nearly completely muzzled patient. To be fair in this matter, I have to compliment the unique conversational talents of the dental hygienists themselves, which are probably more important in supporting this difficult interaction than the patient's side of it. The hygienists seem to have developed unique skills that enable them to understand people who are expressively challenged. With these skills they can somehow interpret, *with great accuracy*, a variety of hand gestures, partially impeded facial expressions, and guttural sounds in order to keep a conversation moving. I find that very impressive. I still do not know how they do it. Unfortunately, we seem to have entered an era where dental patients are allowed to listen to music or watch television with ear phones. I think this is a shameful cop-out and a practice that will eventually lead to the loss of this rare, highly developed, human skill set.

In any case, I found that the whole staff, including the hygienists themselves, to be extremely professional in their concern for my comfort as well as for the results of the treatments. I would always leave with a different suggestion on how to deal with the plaque issue and a bag full of some new type of toothbrush, toothpaste, floss, or rinsing solution. For me it was an hour of interesting conversation with someone of a similar age and interests. I always left with a gift; and the bill arrived well after the fact.

About twenty-four years ago, I met a man at a party who had been working in dental research at the University of Washington. He told me about what was then a relatively new ultrasonic brushing device, which, by now, has become a well-known tool for dental hygiene and is available as the Sonicare toothbrush in virtually every pharmacy. It utilizes ultrasonic waves to enhance the efficiency of plaque removal and, as a consequence, prevents calculus buildup. I thought that this was the answer to my problem and, after being assured that it was not like the ultrasonic cleaner used in the dental office, started to use it as soon as I could get my hands on one. An important aspect of the Sonicare instrument is its timing feature. It gives you two full minutes of "on" time with little blips every thirty seconds, and then it shuts off automatically. I thought it was very cool and that it could rid me of dental plaque issues forever. And from then on, to this very day, I have used that device or one of its descendants faithfully every morning and evening.

In the ensuing years, however, I still required all of the frequently scheduled dental office visits to laboriously chip off tartar from the surfaces of my teeth. After the novelty of using a new, high-tech tool wore off, the actual two-minute experience of tooth brushing felt long and annoying. It seemed like a lot of "psyching up" was required on my part to keep performing my tooth cleaning on a regular twice-a-day-schedule. But I rarely missed or cut short a session, despite developing an ever-increasing dislike for the process.

Another reason for my dislike for the periods of time cleaning my teeth came from my observations of my wife Sheila's dental hygiene practices. It was becoming clear to me that, as I was dutifully applying my scientifically designed and accurately timed 120-second dental cleaning treatments, she was spending less than thirty seconds on hers. I think she used her Sonicare unit for two weeks before putting it back in the box and on the shelf in the closet. Not only that, but she would need to go to the dentist's office for cleanings only every six months, and those sessions would only take fifteen to twenty minutes. The fact that she had more cavities as a kid than I did was rapidly becoming less and less of a consolation. The situation was even more painful given the fact that I could, at moments, stare in awe and amazement at her ridiculously pearly-white, straight teeth.

Matters finally came to a head about fourteen years ago when our dentist retired and we had to go to another office for care.

Upon entering the new dental office, which my wife selected, I was immediately thrown off guard. The sign outside on the street said, "Family and Cosmetic Dentistry." Inside, the walls were painted in colors I could not describe. I only knew that the words "red," "blue," "yellow," "white," "orange," "green," "brown," "black," or any combinations of those did not apply. The artwork did not include any depictions of animal wildlife, rugged mountain peaks, or open desert spaces. There were no *Sports Illustrated*'s among the magazines in the waiting room. All the "before and after" pictures were of smiling women. The dentist was a woman. *Clearly this was not a guy's dentist office.*

I was finally taken back for my examination. I met my new dentist, (a very nice lady who still takes care of my teeth to this day), and her dental hygienist. They examined my teeth. I began to notice that they were exchanging glances that told me they thought *that something was very much amiss*. It is the kind of message that, as a physician, I try not to send to my patients when I think things may be "very much amiss". Finally, after all the recession measurements, the X-rays, and the photographs, my new dentist said something to the effect that I "sure do form *a lot* of tartar on [my] teeth." That, of course, was no big news to me. What happened next was the moment that changed how I live my life.

The nice dentist lady left the room, and I was left with the hygienist, an attractive, twenty-something-year-old. She looked me directly in the eye and said, "Sooo, Dr. Justus, just how often *dooo* you floss and brush your teeth?"

I could tell by the tone of her voice, from her body language, and the way that she accented certain words in that question that she was not really asking me how often I perform dental care.

No, no. *She was really asking me whether or not I floss or brush my teeth at all!*

During the next hour as tartar was being chipped away from my teeth (a task that even required an additional visit to complete), I was overcome with shame.

That was it. I was angry enough to act. I firmly resolved that I was going to vanquish this problem.

I went home and took a look at the Sonicare device sitting on the shelf of the cabinet in my bathroom. This was the machine that was supposed to have solved my excessive plaque problem.

I pulled out the box the Sonicare device came in, took out the instructions, and read them thoroughly (for the first time). I actually learned some things from that.

I started to apply that knowledge in precise ways to my use of the Sonicare. For example, I stopped moving it like a toothbrush over the surface of my teeth and gums. (Something Sheila had pointed out several years before). Also, I used the timing device feature so that I could spend more time in the more plaque-prone areas, such as the lower front teeth. (I experimented with different toothpastes, flossing materials, and mouth rinses. These did not seem to help the situation as much as the cleaning techniques themselves.)

I returned for dental examinations and teeth cleaning on a regular basis. At first, the cleaning procedures would still take most of the hour allotted for these visits and the use of the dreaded ultrasonic cleaner. Now, a few years later, the cleanings can be finished within thirty to forty minutes; I do not require the ultrasonic cleaner; and within a couple of years I was pushed back to a normal, every-six-month visit schedule.

What absolutely shocked me the most was how I felt *right from the start* of my refocused efforts on teeth cleaning with the Sonicare device. I was absolutely absorbed in what I was doing. I felt serene and fulfilled. This was even *before* I had any positive feedback from subsequent dental office visits. What before had been two long minutes of boredom now sped by. What had been dreaded now was happily anticipated. I had this feeling that the two minutes was time that I was experiencing fully. It was not just *living through* these moments to get to the next thing. I knew I wanted more of this feeling in my life but needed to understand it better.

I found myself trying to explain the situation to my wife, other family members, as well as some of the people I work with.

After a few more years of thought, reading on the subject, and exchanging ideas with others, I have come up with the following specific observations on this experience:

The first observation is that the repetition of a non-productive process had created a state of suffering. I was essentially spending four minutes every day of my life in a process that was not achieving the desired goal. I knew this was going on based on my original hygienist's feedback. Yet I kept repeating this same process over and over, fully aware of the fact that it was ineffective. The two minutes twice a day seemed to last longer and longer. I had to force myself to perform the activity. In essence, the time spent in this endeavor had lost its meaning. I believe that this represents the phenomenon referred to by Victor Frankl, the founder of the Viennese school of *logo therapy*, as an "existential void" (i.e., a time spent by a conscious human being that is devoid of meaning for that individual). I would also characterize it as a sort of *mini-neurosis*, given that I had elected to repeat, over and over, an ineffective action. This resulted in a state of suffering, although a relatively brief and mild one. It made me consider how many other neurotic acts I commit in the course of my everyday life, and I was surprised to find out how often that does happen!

Second, the importance of the problem to me was a powerful force. It began with the acquisition of self-knowledge. I became aware of (yet another) personal imperfection. Without this awareness, I would not have experienced the humiliation that comes with being accused of not ever trying to care for my teeth, and I would not have become so focused on trying to improve the process. When the outcome of the process became more important and *took on more meaning*, my focus on the process itself became more intense.

The third observation was that focus on the problem helped clarify the specific role that needed improvement. The process that required improvement was teeth cleaning, more specifically in this case, the operation of the Sonicare device. The operator of that process was me. More precisely, this was the part of "me" that operates the Sonicare, the *Sonicare operator*. It is not the part of me that operates dental floss or the hairbrush or the operator of any other process I control. I think that this distinction is extremely important. It adds objectivity to the whole analysis, and it facilitates the execution of new strategies. Viewing a situation in this way, a person can see him- or herself as defective only in this unique aspect and not generally defective as a person. It keeps the level of shame low by narrowing down the criticism to only a small part or dimension of one's self. For example, one might say, "Oh, I guess I am not such good Sonicare operator, but I am probably a pretty good face washer!" It therefore makes it easier to devise and prescribe more radical changes when the general, overall sense of self is not being assailed and the paralyzing effects of the loss of self-esteem are avoided. It takes much of the emotion out of the situation by making the process more objective. Also, when one is attempting to analyze a more complex process improvement problem, the components will be easier to identify and work on.

The fourth observation was that the physical tool was not useful without the proper utilization systems in place. A tool is most useful when it is used in the most appropriate way. The focus has to be on the performance and therefore the operator's *skill* in the use of the tool. Effective performance cannot be achieved by simply obtaining a more complex or sophisticated device. *The human being operating it has to become more complex or sophisticated* in terms of the skill set that the process of utilization requires.

The design and execution of process change strategies were satisfying even before any goal was achieved. It seems that just the honest attempt to improve the process of teeth cleaning increased the meaning of the time spent in it. In effect, that enhancement of the meaning of the activity of teeth cleaning initiated the "filling in" of the four minutes of existential void that that process had become for me.

The fulfillment associated with the execution of the process persisted after feedback provided indications that the process change was producing results. There was a lingering "halo effect" of satisfaction beyond the two-minute execution. The personal change led to a sense of enhanced self-worth in spite of being a relatively minor personal victory.

CHAPTER 4

MY DEEPER LOOK AT THE SONICARE EXPERIENCE—THE REALIZATION OF THE PHENOMENON OF THE PERSONAL RENAISSANCE EXPERIENCE

From this experience with the treatment of dental plaque, I had sensed that something had happened that was relevant to a basic understanding of personal happiness. I came up with the following analysis that I hoped could help make this personal discovery more broadly applicable to other, more time-consuming roles in my life. My analysis begins with the diagram below (Figure 1). This depicts a specific performance role of mine (the Sonicare operator) using a tool (the Sonicare device) to lead to a desired outcome (teeth free of plaque and tartar).

Figure 1

At baseline, the two minutes spent twice daily had lost their meaning because the ultimate goal was not being achieved. Beyond that, the time spent in the activity felt prolonged and unpleasant; hence it became a state of suffering. By repeating the act over and over for years, it would qualify it as a neurosis, although a relatively minor one.

However, the shame and anger I felt, which resulted from the unspoken condemnation of my teeth cleaning skills by the new dental hygienist, changed the situation. It made me focus on the application of the technique behind the process itself and also helped me find ways that I believed would improve it. In the time that I spent cleaning my teeth and executing newer and better processes, I found myself paying close attention to precise, technical details, hoping to achieve improvements. As I executed these evolving strategies, I would be completely absorbed in the component elements of the act itself—for example, the precise angles at which to apply the bristles on a particular tooth surface or trying to maintain a specific level of pressure. This, in effect, was living in the present without thoughts of the past or the future. (I will discuss my interpretation of the relative importance of past, present, and future time later on.) Essentially, I subsequently learned that I was having the Zen experience of "mindfulness." I think this was part of the reason that the activity was associated with a feeling of such fulfillment.

The goal of the process was restored. The performance of the process became satisfying. The result was a better outcome. In this way, the existential void was filled, and teeth cleaning ceased to be a neurotic act. *Hence, spending four minutes each day on this activity became fulfilling.*

I was experiencing happiness. And although this certainly was not the first time in my life that I felt happy, it was the first time I thought I knew why.

Why was I happy? For me, the real key was the observation I made regarding the first arrow in the following diagram (Figure 2, below): the overall effect of the process improvement on the *operator*.

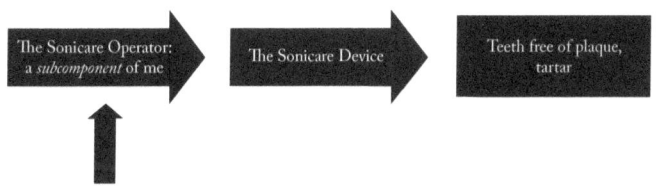

Figure 2

Given that the process *result* had improved, it meant that the operator of the process had to have improved. Specifically, a subcomponent of me, the Sonicare operator, had to improve because the Sonicare device itself remained the same. I have come to view this improvement of self to be a kind of *personal renaissance*, or *rebirth experience*. I believe that this re-creation of a specific, better me is not only a powerfully satisfying experience, but the key element of the experience that engenders happiness.

The film *Groundhog Day* illustrates this. The character played by Bill Murray is introduced to the audience as a shallow, pleasure-seeking, Pittsburgh TV weatherman who is assigned to cover the Groundhog Day ceremony in Punxsutawney, Pennsylvania. He is sexually drawn to a woman on the news crew, Rita, who is portrayed by Andie MacDowell. However, he views the assignment itself as extremely boring and is clearly suffering while carrying it out.

His suffering increases dramatically as he is forced by a surreal twist of fate to repeat the same day over and over until he is driven to attempt suicide. Failing to accomplish this, he finally realizes that this bizarre situation of being forced to live the same day over and over provides him with a series of opportunities to *remake himself* in several distinct ways.

At first, he uses this opportunity to experience relatively shallow pleasures, such as the seduction of an old girlfriend and gaining the upper hand on an old boorish acquaintance. Later on, he learned to play the piano, read French poetry, and finally to become a caring, multi-dimensional individual whom the audience and the beautiful newswoman find very attractive. The audience gets to enjoy the vicarious experience of these multiple personal transformations as much as the main character does. These are essentially multiple personal renaissances in the sense that I described in my situation as the Sonicare operator.

I also believe that once teeth cleaning became a focus for my personal process improvement, it also qualified as a *flow* activity as described by Mihaly Csikszentmihalyi in his book *Flow*. In this book he presents research data on people from all over the world who are from every social-economic stratum and who considered themselves happy. The common characteristic of these people appeared to be that they derived happiness from the execution of personally meaningful, well-defined activities (often their work). These activities had clearly definable goals and, most importantly, *provided challenges that were matched by the skill levels of the people involved.* It was this latter characteristic that was the key factor in helping the participants avoid both boredom (the case where their skill levels *would have been too high for the challenge*) and frustration (where their skill levels *would have been too low for the challenge*). This allowed them to be more fully engaged in the activity ("living in the moment") and to therefore derive a higher level of satisfaction from it. In my case, the goal of plaque removal had suddenly become worthwhile and desirable to me. I participated in defining a plan of action that defined the rules for the process changes I was going to implement. I had the sense that my personal skills were becoming equal to the challenge of teeth cleaning. I also sensed that my concentration was intense while I was executing the plan, and that I was living fully in those moments with no thoughts of the past or fears of the future. Therefore, self-consciousness in those moments was not an interfering factor. The time spent in the activity seemed to speed by, when before it seemed interminable. The feedback came from my observation of the amount of time required in subsequent dental office visits to clean my teeth of tartar. In Csikszentmihalyi's view, people who have flow experiences achieve happiness at those times without actually pursuing it directly. He also points out that this is in agreement with the conclusion of the English philosopher John Stuart Mill, who asserted that happiness *ensues* from certain actions. I agree completely with this conclusion. My next question was how could one apply this information to other situations and live a happier life? There will be more on this later.

There is another way to look at this kind of personal transformation. Most people acknowledge that there is something very satisfying about creating a work of art. At some time in our lives most of us have done this in some form: made a finger painting in kindergarten, carved some object from wood, made up a song, wrote a story or poem, or even just built a sand castle on the beach. Surely anyone who has done this can remember a feeling of satisfaction building within them during the creative act and reaching a climax just afterwards as they admired their finished work. I believe that the essence of any artistic endeavor is the transformation of some physical element that, at baseline, has either very little or no meaning into an entity that has greater meaning. For example, a sculptor takes a block of marble and chips it away until it is transformed into the image of a biblical figure; a composer arranges symbols in a very specific pattern on a piece of paper that represent sounds of varying pitch and duration, the result of which is a beautiful symphony; the writer arranges symbols representing the sounds of a language in a specific way on blank sheets of paper that, when read by others, convey a story. In each of these cases a transformation occurs: a change from the relative chaos and resultant lack of meaning of the materials used (random symbols, paints, a block of granite, grains of sand) into a more *ordered* product that expresses a more specific meaning. This meaning, in turn, is capable of evoking a very specific set of ideas or emotions in others who witness the product.

When we improve ourselves as an operator of any process, we essentially become an artist who, working with elements of his or her own thoughts and actions, *changes oneself in a very specific way,* from a state of relative chaos to one of relative order. And we, as the controllers of these processes, experience the same sense of fulfillment that the artist experiences when he converts a block of stone into a stunning representation of a person.

There is no better way to illustrate the concept of the creative process, the transition from chaos to order, and its effect on the persons creating order out of chaos than in the recent and extremely popular Netflix reality show called "Tidying Up with Marie Kondo". Marie is a charming, young Japanese woman who visits the very untidy homes of people whose closets, kitchens, bathrooms, bedrooms, garages are cluttered with excess clothing and other possessions and who have decided to accept help. She urges them to only keep items that "spark joy" and get rid of the rest. She passes on a variety of tips on how to store things. For example, she teaches them how to maximize the efficiency of sock storage that include a specific way to fold and place them in a drawer. What happens in the homes of these formerly messy people is *literally* a transition from chaos to order. It is obvious from the comments they make at the conclusion of the episode that "joy" is not only "sparked" by the items that they decide to keep. It is also "sparked" by the process of becoming better organizers of their possessions.

In any case, I knew there was something very good about the Sonicare experience. I certainly felt happy doing it. If the two minutes I spent twice a day in this apparently mundane activity were that fulfilling, I wanted to have more minutes like them. I knew that I regularly lived through periods of time in my day-to-day life that felt more like my dental care time before the focus on process improvement. There were indeed too many "existential voids." I felt that there were periods of time of variable lengths that I felt I was *living through*, rather than *living in*. It was as if I just tolerated them so that I could get to some other experience, although I did not actually remember having made this bargain consciously. I felt truly fulfilled in the four minutes of dental care that I was now performing and wanted the other 1,336 minutes of the day to feel the same.

CHAPTER 5

EXAMINATION OF MY DAILY ROLES

I believed that my Sonicare experience had provided me with keys to living a more fulfilling life. One of these was the observation that it had made me feel more connected with my environment. Specifically, I had become aware of a relatively minor environmental challenge (in this case, what mouth bacteria and other factors can do to the surface of my teeth), and then devised and executed a strategy to deal with it. One could call this experience an example of *adaptive behavior*. By adaptive behavior, I mean activity that could help a person better cope with the challenges he or she faces in the world. These would be characterized by recognizing an opportunity to improve some outcome in a specific process, gathering relevant environmental information, and then effecting changes in the process that would likely improve the outcome. (In following chapters I will present the reasons why I believe this kind of activity *should be* associated with feelings of happiness and why we in highly developed societies tend to be, to varying degrees, oblivious to these opportunities.) In my Sonicare experience, I discovered a way to make a satisfying life change in a very specific role. The next challenge for me was to see how to accomplish this more often in other areas of my life. I began a review of my daily roles to identify the associated specific processes that I could address in a manner analogous to the dental hygiene process. I initially came up with the information depicted in Figure 3.

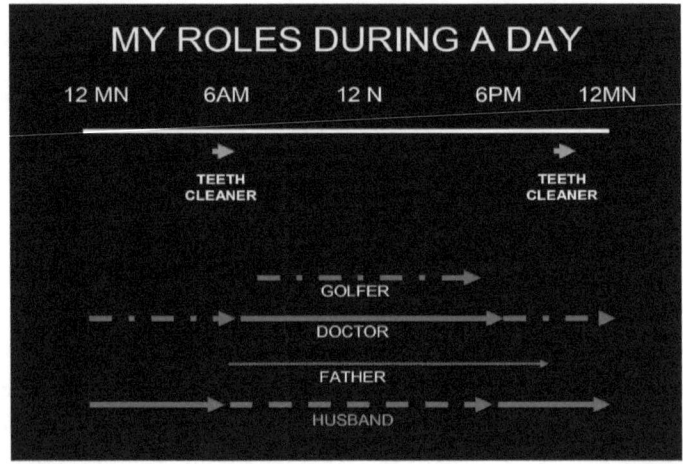

Figure 3

I wanted to focus on roles that occupied more of my time. I wanted a bigger bang for my personal-process-improvement buck, so to speak. The graph above depicts the roles in which I spend the most amounts of time during the course of a regular day. They are my professional role as a physician, as well as my personal roles as a father and a husband. I threw in the golfer role to illustrate some specific points that I will make within the next few pages. (Also,

I happen to enjoy golf.) The dots or dashes indicate that the time I actually spend performing each role in a given day or week. Those time commitments vary. For example, since my children do not live at home anymore and we are usually not together at night, my father role is smaller than it used to be. I am at work in the doctor role for most days of the week during the day, with occasional night calls. In my husband role, I am most always at home with my wife during the nights and on most weekend days. I am a golfer for a few hours once or twice a week depending on the weather or sometimes in spite of it.

As I looked for a process to improve that was connected with these roles, I was struck by the fact that each of these roles is extremely complex and actually composed of many sub-roles. It would take a long time to specifically identify all of them. (I have come to the conclusion that it is not actually important to identify *all* the sub-roles because one really does not have enough time to focus on all of them anyway. There will be more on that later.) Nevertheless, I made efforts to employ the lessons I learned from improving my Sonicare operator role in at least some of the processes associated with the other, more time-consuming roles I have.

CHAPTER 6

LESSONS FROM GOLF

Note to the Reader: Do not skip this chapter because you do not happen to like golf! This chapter is *very important* in terms of understanding of how to take advantage of opportunities for happiness in life. You may actually want to take up golf after reading this. At least you will understand the people who have done so and who are passionate about it. There is a reason why there is a whole network devoted to this sport, and *it is not the same reason* why there is a whole network devoted to shopping at home.

I learned a great deal about personal process improvement from the attention I directed to my *golfer* role. Golf is a good example to use because it encompasses a finite number of fairly easily recognized, specific processes.

Golf could be played as a social activity where, for example, one can drink beer in the company of friends, schmooze your boss, or advance some business interest. However, *if one's desire is to get better at it*, golf becomes a quintessential personal improvement activity and, as such, multiple personal renaissance experiences.

To better understand this, please consider this fictional scenario: There is an evil golf god who wants to torment a real golfer *in the worst way*. How would they go about that? In my opinion they would do one of two things: Analogous to the Greek legend of Sisyphus (the guy who was condemned by the gods to keep rolling a huge rock up a hill only to see it roll right back down every time he got it close to the top), the evil golf god could allow the golfer to advance the ball onto the green and roll the ball toward the hole. But each time the ball approached its target, it would take a big U-turn and be flung back onto the tee box, or starting point, of the same hole. Or, even more relevant to the point of this book, this same evil god (who, by the way, actually does exist) could make it so that whenever the golfer played a round, he or she would score on his or her first stroke of every hole so that the standard, eighteen-hole game score would be eighteen every time. Although this might be fun for a round or two, it would eventually make the experience meaningless. It would become meaningless because there would be no way for the player to create a better outcome than one represented by a score of eighteen. Constantly striving to create a better outcome is the key to deriving satisfaction from playing the game of golf and, I believe, playing the game of life as well. (By the way, the evil golf god figured out that creating either of the two conditions described above would just limit the number of golfers he or she could torment, so the god instead uses other techniques, such as the *snap hook* and the dreaded *shank*, that do not necessarily discourage participation to the same degree.)

Golf is an individual sport, and therefore it is entirely personal. There are no teammates with whom to share success and failure on the course (except to some degree in the professional game where players have their own personal caddies, coaches, and physical trainers). Stroke numbers are measurable. The object is to complete eighteen holes of play in the fewest number of strokes possible. Golf, in fact, is difficult. It is very unlikely that any currently recognized human being will ever shoot a perfect score of eighteen on any regulation eighteen-hole course. A calculation of the average number of strokes per game over a period of time, compared with an objective standard of excellence (i.e., a golfer's handicap), tells the person where he or she is as golfer relative to any other competitor with a handicap in the world. This number is available to players and updated shortly after completion of the last round played. It serves as an indication of the golfer's proficiency at any point in time and therefore can provide a measure of both improvements and declines. Resources for self-improvement are plentiful—instructional books, videos, access to teaching professionals, driving ranges, and psychologists, all provide golfers with instructions for improving their golf games.

I realized from the tooth brushing experience that identifying a precise process was critical in making real, positive changes. I found again that it was important to focus on the *processor*, that is, the individual executing the involved processes, and define that role in the most detailed way possible. Defining the processor as *the golfer*, per se, does not help a player improve their golf game. There are many different processes that golfers will need to learn and improve for their scores and handicaps to improve. Figure 4 below illustrates this point. Most people who have played golf at least once will realize that to move the ball from the tee area into the hole on the green, requires the execution of different kinds of shots. These would include the tee shot, the full-swing approach shot, sometimes the pitch shot or chip shot, and the putt. The focus of these activities should not be primarily the specific clubs involved or the ball. The focus should be on the executor of these maneuvers: the "tee-shot maker," the "full-approach shot maker," the "pitch-shot maker," the "chip-shot maker," and the "put maker." As one works on these sub-roles of the golfer, the game scores and handicaps decrease, and one is then reborn in these specific ways. To keep improving, it becomes obvious that the player must recognize that all of these sub-roles themselves have relevant sub-sub-roles illustrated by the empty bubbles in Figure 4 whose identification are the keys to future, overall game improvement.

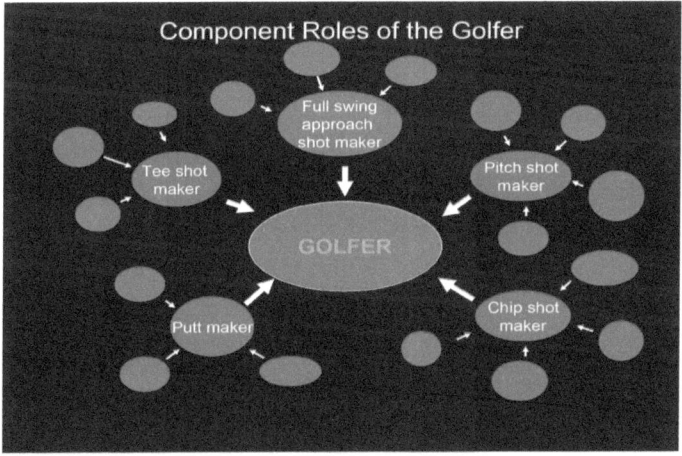

Figure 4

For example, the "full-swing approach shot maker" has component roles (not labeled in the illustration above) that include a low-draw hitter, a high-draw hitter, a low-cut hitter, a high-cut hitter, and so on. An understanding of these complexities leads to the improvements. The professional golfer would have a game reflective of varying degrees of understanding and mastery of all of these sub-component roles.

By applying this understanding, I have been able to reduce my handicap over the last few years. I find all the time that I am engaged in hitting balls on the driving range and practice greens; that is, the personal process improvement of the *tee-shot maker, full-swing maker*, and so on is just as fulfilling as my practice experience as the Sonicare operator. The personal renaissance feeling is basically the same. The time I spend either in practice or in a game passes all too quickly.

I approach golf with the same basic mental premise as the other things I do: I acknowledge that I am not now as good as I could be at any of these sub-component golfer roles. Therefore, the impression I have of myself in the role of, for example, the *putt maker*, is relevant only as a point of baseline information from which I can devise and execute strategies to make improvements. I have no previously constructed image of myself as a golfer to live up to. I am relieved of the shackles of self-consciousness, free to live in the current moments of a process change activity.

All this activity is propelled by believing in the goal of improving golf game scores and the handicap. Put another way, the game is not about seeing the ball land in a receptacle that has been placed just below ground level somewhere on a patch of ground covered with very short grass. It is about changing the characteristics of the physical actions that propel it to that location, as well as the mental decisions that occur just before the execution of those physical actions. This means that the activity of practice (i.e., the improvement of those physical actions) has meaning, and it is therefore not time just to be *lived through*; rather, it is time to be *fully lived in*. There is no existential void during those minutes and hours spent practicing and playing the game. Each time the process improves, the processor experiences the glowing, positive feeling of a personal renaissance.

Successful athletes in other sports are always attributing good outcomes to attention to process. The sport sections of your local paper are probably full of this assertion. The Seattle Times quoted Russell Wilson, the quarterback of the NFL Seahawks, who was asked about how he was going to approach the offseason after a better than expected finish in 2018 that ended with an early playoff loss:

> "I think (of) having a great offseason…I think (of) preparing at the highest level; there's only one way to do it and that's got to be your mentality, that's got to be the way that you go after everything, *the attention to detail, how you prepare.* Getting together with each guy as much as each player can get around each other and just throwing footballs, catching and *having a lot of fun while doing it.*" (The italics are mine.)

In this statement, Russell Wilson, an accomplished athlete, a Super Bowl champion, not only echoes the importance of process improvement in his sport but also asserts that those specific activities *engender* happiness.

There is another critical point to bring into this discussion. The late Arnold Palmer is an icon in the sport of golf. He was a multiple major tournament champion.

His swashbuckling style endeared himself to many people and was a major factor in promoting and popularizing the sport throughout the world just as Tiger Woods has done in recent years. In his heyday, he would be followed by thousands of spectators ("Arnie's Army") waiting to witness one of his late, heroic charges and win a big tournament on the last few holes. Mr. Palmer played well as he aged. In 1995, in one of the rounds of a Senior golf tour event in the Seattle area, he was well under par, "shooting his age" on his 66th birthday. However, after that, the passage of time finally did catch up with him and his game deteriorated. It was hard for me having seen him in his prime, to watch him play on various Golf Channel events, not being the same player that he was. He remained a beloved figure in and out of the game through his involvement with big tournaments (including his own) and because of his well-known philanthropy. Over the last few years, his life was celebrated in several Golf Channel biographies. In one of them he mentioned that he still practiced golf on a regular basis. When asked why, he gave a simple but revealing answer, something to the effect that *"I just want to get better."* So, this player had reached a point in his life where practicing at golf would not in any way elevate his game to a level that would make him competitive again at the professional level. Yet, there was still this drive to keep working to become a better golfer. This supports the idea that the pursuit of self-improvement is satisfying no matter from where you are starting or where you have been at any point in the past. And that satisfaction does not depend on the achievement of any specific level of improvement. It is all about knowing where one is at any particular "now", having a concept of what one can do to move in a positive direction from that "now", and then executing that concept.

By the way, this chapter could have been about painting a wall, driving a nail, driving a race car, playing a musical instrument, building a house, carving wood, performing a heart transplantation, or being a friend. I hope you get the idea!

What I try to do now is employ the basic elements of the approach described above to everything else I do in life. However, to understand how that might work, I had to come to an understanding of why a person would derive satisfaction from personal process improvement. I felt that the answer lay in an analysis of the essence of life itself.

CHAPTER 7

THE BIOLOGIC IMPERATIVES

We all know that we human beings are just one of many forms of life that exist in the world. Being members of this club, we have characteristics in common, to varying degrees, with all other living entities. That is the reason that I am bringing Biology, the study of life, into the discussion of human happiness. Biologic discoveries lead us to better understandings of the functions of living organisms. This information then can lead us to an understanding of the general purpose of life itself. So, in the case of us human beings, once we understand our biologic purpose, we are closer to knowing which of our controllable activities carry the most meaning for us, at least in the biologic sense. Then, *knowing which processes have the greatest meaning for us, allows us to better target activities that most merit the investment of time in potential process-improvement strategies.*

Now, I know that some of you readers are dismissing this line of thinking because you view our species, Homo sapiens, as group so distinct from other living organisms that it would be crazy to think there could be some common thread of purpose among all living entities. I would just ask you to read on for a small infusion of humility.

So, how does a biologic approach to the question of the purpose of life actually work? Look at it this way: Let's say an alien spaceship lands in Central Park in New York City, and its occupants drop off a complex-looking object and depart without giving any kind of explanation. What would be your first question? Most likely it would be something like, "What is this thing for? *What is its purpose?*" How would you begin to answer that question? All you have to do is remember how this situation is approached in the science fiction movies: the authorities move in, cordon off the area, and either contain the object in some quickly erected structure or carry it off to some large building in a military facility. There, a large number of scientific personnel in white coats, armed with all kinds of impressive-looking devices, begin the process of carefully examining its components. All of this would be done to determine their contribution to the object's overall function and, thereby, identify the purpose of the alien machine.

So, it is logical that a similar approach, that is an examination of the structure and function of the components that make up living things, would help us gain a better understanding of the general purpose of life. But, because there are huge differences between the outward appearances of many of these living beings (e.g., a single streptococcus bacterium versus an elephant), we, like the scientists in white coats, are going to have to look very deeply, with very sophisticated microscopic and biochemical tools, to get this information.

Let's continue this discussion with the following question: "In the most basic sense, what *functional characteristic* distinguishes living organisms from the non-living entities that occupy this planet?" I believe that it is the function of *self-replication*. Whatever living entity you can mention—big or little, simple or complex, singe cell or multicellular, plant or animal—they all do it. Non-living matter does not.

Self-replication (reproduction) begins when DNA (deoxyribonucleic acid), a complex molecule invisible to the human eye (see Figure 5 below), makes a copy of itself. All forms of life are either incomplete or complete single cells (e.g., viruses and bacteria) or they are the integration of many cells (multicellular organisms, e.g. us). At the core of every one of these cells resides a full copy of the DNA molecule that is specific for that particular individual living entity. The DNA molecule carries all the information that went into creating that entity and sustaining its existence. Put another way, DNA produces the materials that determine how the complete life form looks and how it acts. Therefore, for example, in the case of the simplest, microscopic ones, such as viruses, the new copy of DNA, or, occasionally, a similar molecule called RNA (ribonucleic acid) will generate a life form that looks exactly like the one it came from. In more complicated, multicellular organisms that reproduce sexually, the copies of DNA come from two different individuals, and the offspring will have features of both parent organisms.

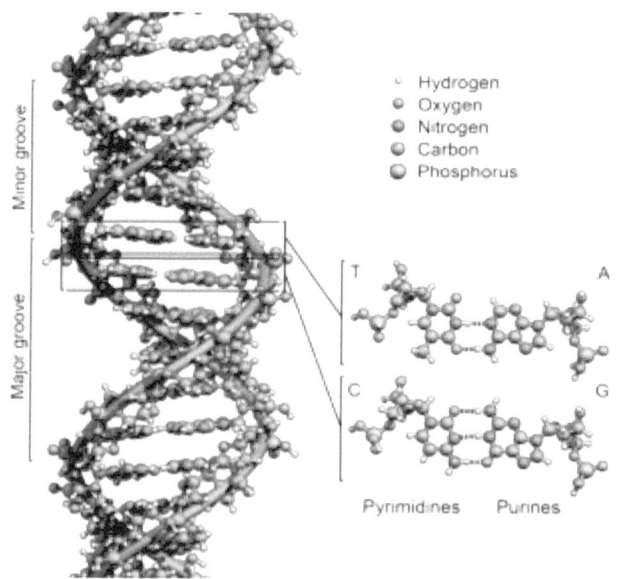

Figure 5—A small, vastly magnified segment of a DNA molecule.

In essence, the evolution of both the single-cell and the multicellular organisms found in the world today depended on two factors: the first one is that the molecular structures of their DNA have been, for various reasons, changing over time; and the second is that these changes had resulted in organisms whose structural and functional characteristics favored their survival over their environmental competitors. If a particular organism did survive, the likelihood that the evolving central DNA "master" molecule could continue to replicate itself was increased.

The evolution of multicellular organisms features an interesting development called cell specialization. This means that specific groups of cells (organs) perform distinct functions for the overall benefit of the whole organism. As multicellular organisms passed through the evolutionary process, survival and reproduction were enhanced through improvements in nutrient acquisition and utilization, mobility, defense, waste handling, and information gathering and processing systems. Another result of cell differentiation and specialization is cell and organ interdependency. Expressed in the language of economics, this means the cells would trade products or services with each other for their overall benefit. This will be discussed in another context later.

As I mentioned, over eons, there have been continual changes in the biochemical structure of the various forms of DNA. The result has been, over a span of three to four billion years, a proliferation of life forms from the isolated, molecular precursors of current-day DNA molecules to the single-cell organism, and finally, to the more complex life forms, like us, *Homo sapiens*. You can think of this like the evolution of computer software: it started with DNA, version 1.0, and we human beings now have DNA, version gazillion.gazillion. No doubt, barring some major catastrophe, this process will continue. Ever since the completion of the Human Genome Project in which the chemical structure of our DNA was completely defined, scientists have been able to trace the evolution of our species from others through comparisons of critical areas of DNA. It turns out that regions of DNA that code for the production of proteins ("the building blocks of life" – as you probably remember from your Biology class) are remarkably similar to corresponding areas in other species. Dr. Francis S. Collins, a leader of the Human Genome Project, commented in his book, "The Language of God", that the protein-coding zones of DNA from a Chimpanzee are exactly the same as ours; a dog is a 99% match; mouse 99%; Chicken 73%; fruit fly 60%; and a roundworm 35%. These differences reflect the distance in evolutionary terms between Homo sapiens and these animals. Maybe this information should make us humbler as a species. At least it makes answering the old cartoon question, "Are you a man or a mouse?" more problematic. Feeling humbler yet?

OK, now let's review this in more detail. We can imagine the first versions of DNA as much simpler molecules than current-day human DNA, floating in a water environment. Then, over many years of DNA replication, the molecule changes, resulting in the more complex forms of DNA that have been responsible for the vast varieties of living entities that exist in the water and on the land today. In the first stages of this amazing series of events, there would be the acquisition of a covering material or membrane, providing protection for activities of these strands of this early, relatively simple form of DNA. This newly-evolved structure would eventually become the first version of the *living cell*. In other words, within the now-protected, watery environment of the cell, DNA could more reliably make copies of itself and direct the functions of the cell. Subsequently, over eons, new alterations in DNA resulted in continued changes in cell structure and function. These changes in cell structure and function, in turn, increased the likelihood of cell survival, and that would also increase the chance that those newer forms of DNA would replicate. Single-cell organisms would evolve with more complex cell walls. Certain specialized, cell wall structural enhancements provided improvements of mobility. Other mutations of DNA would result in functional changes that would help them consume more varied sources of nutrients, including other life forms. Later, multicellular organisms appeared that featured interdependent groups of specialized cells. Also, much later, subsequent alterations in DNA allowed newer, multi-cellular iterations of this evolutionary process to leave the water and exploit environmental niches on land and still have the ability to carry out water-based biochemical functions without essentially dying from drying out. As a mental exercise, think of yourself as a collection of 35 to 40 trillion aquaria all stuck together! These and other changes have allowed living entities to become increasingly more effective exploiters of the Earth's resources.

So, differences in the structure of DNA account for the observable differences between living things. Periodic changes in DNA structure result in alterations of the appearance and function of the organism in which the DNA is housed. These basic changes in DNA, which may or may not occur by accident (depending on where you stand on the issue of "intelligent design"), either end up favoring the organism's survival or favoring its extinction. The achievement of long-term biologic success simply means that the organism had sufficient opportunities to replicate itself, and extinction means that it did not. It does not matter how great or small or how simple or complex the organism is. What is important is how well it can exploit the environmental niche in which it resides. The alterations in DNA structure simply have to result in changes in the organism's functional characteristics which favor an enhancement of reproductive opportunities. That is just how natural selection works.

So, if you placed a human being side-by-side with a rock and said the *essential* difference between the two entities was that one has arms and legs and the other doesn't, I would say you were incorrect. Arms and legs can amuse us as we watch their owners using them in a variety of ways (basketball, ballet, and so on). However, their basic purpose is to make humans more efficient gatherers of energy sources. Energy is required to run all the body's systems that preserve and extend the life of that individual, and that, in turn, increases reproductive opportunities and therefore reproductive success. You could have also said it was the brain and its sensory extensions (elements of the nervous system). I would also allow that the brain and sensory organs are distinctive structures that provide amusing, pleasurable activities. We can enjoy the sensory input provided by music concerts, sexual activity, good-tasting food, massages, and more. We can also delight in the mental images evoked by theatrical performances, dance recitals, and motion pictures. However, I believe that the most important function of the senses, from the viewpoint of life's essential function (*the preservation of a specific molecule of DNA through time*) is to support survival and reproductive activity. By assembling the information that the senses gather and making an assessment of the environment based on this information, the mind can then devise strategies to gain easier access to sources of energy and to avoid ambient threats. Both of these activities enhance survival, which, in turn, increases the number of reproductive opportunities. If this were not the case, we would not have had the requisite luxury of time and resources to invent and utilize movie theaters, auditoriums, stadiums, restaurants, brothels, magazines, or, for that matter, to buy chocolate cake or heroin.

By the way, I do not intend to demean all the activities mentioned above, with the exception of the ones (like taking heroin) that are obviously harmful. Sports and the performing arts certainly have very significant value for the individuals who practice them. They all are examples of personal process improvement along the lines I described in the previous chapter on golf. Watching those who can carry them out at the highest levels can be experientially enriching. However, I strongly believe it is better for the individual to be the player or performer, no matter what his or her level of skill or achievement happens to be, than to be the observer. Playing games is, in essence, just an exercise of various sets of skills that have potential use in activities more directly associated with attempts to survive and prosper. Therefore, participating in those games carries more intrinsic meaning for us than simply observing skills exercised by others.

Arms, legs, ears, eyes, heads, brains, and nerves are distinctive-looking and sophisticated tools that are produced and maintained through the direction of DNA, and they serve to promote DNA's replication. I think the key structural difference between all living things and the rock I mentioned earlier is that some of the atoms that make up living entities are arranged into DNA molecules. Although molecules of DNA differ from one organism to the next, they all share one common goal. That goal is to preserve the organism's existence over long periods of time through self-replication. Rocks are relatively stable bits of matter, but they do not actively attempt to reproduce themselves. Even if they happen to be as impressive looking as Mount Everest, they don't do that.

One could view this situation of preserving genetic information through time as *de facto* attempts to achieve physical immortality.

The pursuit of this goal best defines life in the physical sense. There is no scientific or logical reason that groups of atoms should behave in this way. Why couldn't they just be happy and behave like the arrangement of atoms that make up rocks? They could just sit around and wait to be blown by the wind, eroded by the flow of water, or bombarded by some extraterrestrial form of energy. For me, the improbability that chance alone set all this in motion has helped firm up my belief in a higher power. (The other factors relate to the pursuit of spirituality immortality, which I will discuss later.)

So, DNA directs the construction of all the physical elements that are found in any living entity. These elements are designed and maintained in a way to enhance the success of DNA's central mission of self-replication. This is what distinguishes living beings from all other things in the world. This helps explain some perplexing things that happen in our world, which I will discuss in subsequent chapters, and also provides the philosophical basis for a way to derive more satisfaction (hence happiness) from life.

Another key point to emphasize is the importance of efficiency in energy acquisition. Living entities, in the competitive environment of our world, not only have to possess the tools to exploit their niches, but would be best served if the amount of energy *expended while obtaining energy resources* is relatively low. (It clearly *cannot exceed* the amount of energy gained. That would be a doomed "business model" from the "get-go" for that life form!) Stated another way, the less energy expenditure that is required while obtaining a given amount of energy, the *greater the net gain* in energy. And the greater the net gain in energy, the greater the potential for survival. As I will point out later, this is one of the most important driving forces in the establishment and evolution of societal groups.

This is not just true for us human beings, but also for all living beings. For example, our house is surrounded by several species of birds. My wife Sheila feeds them on a regular basis. One of the birds is a beautiful, blue creature with a black head called the Steller's jay (pictured below in Figure 6).

Figure 6

Sheila throws them a handful of peanuts in shells when she sees a group of them (generally two or three) gathered in the trees and large bushes in the garden outside our kitchen. They will fly down, one at a time, to the patio to look at the whole-shell nuts scattered on the ground. They invariably will pick them up one at time and shake them, apparently testing their relative weights, as they seem to prefer the "doubles" or "triples" over the single nuts. Then they pack their mouths and beaks with as many as they can carry before flying off. This type of behavior is much like the smart shopper who picks the largest items rather than the smaller ones that are sold individually in the fruit and vegetable department at the grocery store. The bird is essentially increasing the efficiency of this energy-gathering, life-maintaining process by making sure each energy-consuming and potentially dangerous decent from the relative safety of their perches above the open ground results in the maximum return of energy gained.

This activity, when played out in the human arena, has had both positive and negative implications. In human socioeconomic terms, the admired winner at this game is a capitalist (or more likely in our times, a collection of capitalists) who, acting within the norms of the overall social group, creates a product that others perceive as better and desirable. This results in a market for that product and economic opportunities for others working directly and indirectly in that market. On the other hand, when people pursue efficiencies in energy acquisition *outside* accepted norms (e.g., bank robbery, Ponzi schemes, exchanges of economic power for votes, or other forms of political corruption) can be the result.

The next issue that requires examination is how pursuits of physical immortality over time have affected the evolution of the social systems that help shape our lives. This will be addressed in the next chapter.

CHAPTER 8

THE EVOLUTION OF BIOLOGIC AND SOCIAL ORGANISMS

It is interesting how closely the organizational patterns of social groups resemble the organization of the cellular components of the individual, human organisms that compose those groups. This relationship was initially described by a 19th century English scientist and philosopher, Herbert Spencer, who is better known for coining the term "survival of the fittest". For example, as I mentioned in the previous chapter, a human being has organs (that is, groups of specialized cells) that help in the gathering of nutrients (e.g., the musculoskeletal system), their consumption and absorption (the digestive system), and their distribution (the circulatory system), while societies have, respectively, farmers, food processors, food transport systems, and grocery stores. The body has a defensive system that consists of a protective outer layer of skin and aggressive internal agents (the immune system) that, respectively, block the entry of potential invaders and detect and kill perceived foreign cells and disable other foreign substances. Similarly, societies have built border walls, missile defense systems, and have weapon-wielding military personnel. The human organism has special systems to rid itself of waste products (e.g., the kidneys and liver) while societies have waste-management systems, such as garbage trucks and sewage treatment plants. A human being has fatty tissue to store energy and the society has refrigerators, freezers, and banks to store currency with which to purchase energy for the bodies of its constituents. The person has recognition and intolerance of non-self-entities (a critical characteristic of the immune system—see below for more details), while the social group talks in various ways about "protecting its own", "border security", "defense of the homeland", etc. It is not an accident that, facing the same environmental challenges, the functional elements of a social group would be similar to those of the collection of cells that make up each of its individual members.

It is worthwhile to dwell a bit longer on the similarities of the body's defense system to those that exist in society since they have a direct bearing on the origins of certain moral, religious, and ethical tenets. As I just mentioned, multicellular organisms have certain specialized cells that act as defenders of the whole organism and thereby are at risk to be sacrificed for the sake of protecting it. Cells of the immune system are created to be casualties, for example, in the process of repelling the attack of invading bacteria. The analogous elements of human societal self-sacrifice would be military personnel, policemen, firemen, or all heroic human beings who act selflessly in the defense of other members of their group.

A very important element in this process for both the living, individual organism and the societal organism is the determination of *to what* (in the case of the former) *and to whom* (in the case of the latter) we should direct this protective activity. In practically every multicellular organism, there is the characteristic of the recognition of foreign elements as "*self*", versus those that are "*non-self*". Each organism is programmed to deal harshly with *non-self*-elements but to tolerate those which are *self*. This "immune recognition" element is an important early step in the process used by many multicellular organisms to protect themselves from invasion by foreign entities, such as bacteria or viruses. (By the way, certain failures in this system cause allergic conditions as well as the so-called "autoimmune diseases," such as rheumatoid arthritis, Crohn's disease, and systemic lupus erythematosus.) In our societal interactions, we also have the concept of tolerance of others, e. g., "love thy neighbor as thyself", and intolerance, (you can fill in the blank): "They are just a bunch of ...."), which are important factors in, respectively, the resolution and in the perpetuation of social conflict. Understanding this is a key element in achieving personal happiness as a member of any social group. I will discuss this in different contexts in some of the chapters that follow.

There are other comparisons that have implications for understanding economics and politics. More complex, multicellular organisms are made up of several, functionally distinct collections of cells, called organs. Each organ provides a specific service. Essentially, all the different organs are functionally interdependent as each one plays a vital role in the survival of the whole organism. For example, a certain group of muscle cells (part of the musculoskeletal system) can cause the chest cavity to expand, which pulls oxygen containing air into the lungs—a part of the respiratory system. In turn, this brings oxygen close to oxygen-depleted red blood cells so the oxygen can be attached to the hemoglobin molecule inside the red blood cells, which belong to the hematologic system. The heart then pushes these oxygen-rich red blood cells through blood vessels in the circulatory system to all the organs of the body, where the oxygen is released and then taken up by the cells that make up those structures. The oxygen is used to generate the energy that enables the cells in the body to perform their life-sustaining tasks, including the groups of muscles that brought the oxygen into the lungs in the first place. The kidney cells, part of the genitourinary system, also require oxygen to do their work to remove some of the potentially poisonous by-products that result from the use of energy as well as the other metabolic processes of these specialized cell systems. Each component of the body essentially trades its service with other components for the mutual benefit of the whole organism.

In social organizations, the same dynamic exists. Remember when your grandparents, or more likely now your great-grandparents, talked about where they shopped? They might have referred to these specific places as where they "traded." A "trade" was another word for a specific job (i.e., a specialized societal function, such as a carpenter, bricklayer, or an electrician). This term came from even earlier times when people actually would trade their products or services directly with those who provided other products or services. Of course, these days, we use a device that is supposed to represent the value of these exchanged products and services: *money*. (See a later chapter for more on money and possessions as they relate to happiness, per se.) In any case, successful societies have the pervasive trait of functional interdependency just like successful biologic systems.

Living organisms that are made up of interdependent organ systems die if the exchange of biological services and products fails, and societal systems fail for basically the same reason.

Are these similarities some kind of accident? I do not think so.

I do not think so because the factor that brings an individual into a social group is the same that favored the evolution of multicellular organisms from single-cell life forms in the first place. *Integrated specialization* provides at least the potential for greater efficiency in life-sustaining, environmental exploitation. This is true for both *an individual* multicellular organism as well as for *a group* of multicellular organisms. Many different species of animals, such as bees, wolves, apes, ants, bears, lions, and crows, have obviously come to this same conclusion. With regard to our species, I believe that there was a time when a few individual, genetically similar hominids (human-like creatures) decided to join together for reasons other than the promotion of opportunities for sexual intercourse. This was done to gain a survival advantage for themselves and their offspring. Improvements in survival increased the chances for successful, repetitive reproduction. If this trend toward enlarging social groups had not provided that survival advantage, we would not be seeing the pervasive pattern of social integration and the rising population of human beings that exist in the world today. I do not think that the basic motivation has changed since then.

The members of a social group face the same sort of challenges in the environment that individual cells faced when environmental factors favored their association in a multicellular organism. Social groups could be expected to evolve over time along the same general lines: segments of the population perform specialized tasks, such as sheltering, acquiring energy, passive and aggressive defensive functions, disposing of waste products, and so on. But again, all this exists to satisfy the individuals who had "joined up" with the expectation that they would derive a survival benefit.

Which functional component of societal evolution is analogous to that of DNA in biologic evolution? I believe it is consciousness. Decisions that are made by the conscious mind and shared between minds determine the structure and function of social groups just as DNA controls the structure and function of the *living* entity in which it is housed. Just as in biologic evolution, societies cannot make effective adaptations to the environment without at least some individuals alone or in relatively small groups coming up with *alternative concepts* of societal structure that result in new social constructs that might function better than the ones they replace.

It is my belief that the creation of these "mutational" events in the "DNA" of our consciousness have the ability to evoke positive, reinforcing feelings in the individuals who conceive them, *even before* they are proven to be of benefit. As you may remember, I proved this to myself when I felt the feelings of fulfillment when I just started to apply process improvement techniques to teeth cleaning, well before the new techniques were validated by subsequent dental checkups. A more important example of this would be that of Thomas Edison's development of the light bulb. By the late 1870's, he had already determined that electrical current, passed through a filament in vacuum, would provide a relatively long-lasting source of light, but he needed to find the best filament material. He found that carbonized plant matter would fill this role but needed to test over 6,000 vegetable materials before settling on carbonized cotton. Even then, he needed many more experiments to refine the design that led to his patent in 1880. What would have kept him going after testing plant material #3,436 and preparing to test #3,437? I believe that all the failed experiments as well as the ultimate successful one had meaning for him because of a strong belief in the overall goal. Each of those experiments represented an opportunity to live fully in the present and experience the satisfying sensations of mindfulness. They all were suitable tests for his skill as an inventor and they all provided opportunities to improve those skills. And, not incidentally, with the final success of this project came the confirmation of his improvement in the "inventor" sub-role of his life.

It is, however, important to point out that there are several pitfalls for individuals when they associate with others and form any kind of social organization. For example, what if the expectations that each party holds are not met? The social arrangement can easily fall apart if enough of the individuals involved feel that they are not receiving the survival advantage afforded by their participation or when they feel that other parties involved are not holding up their ends of the bargain. There could be many reasons why this could happen, such as sickness, injury, and environmental change. Also, society itself can create opportunities for people to *perversely* exercise something along the lines of the phenomenon that I mentioned earlier of maximizing the efficiency of energy acquisition by minimizing the consumption of energy used to obtain it. A current socio-political example of this is the provision of an entitlement through a government-directed initiative where the alternative for the beneficiary, (in this case, an otherwise capable, rich or poor individual), would be to work more directly for the asset themselves. This could include welfare abuse as well as the creation of laws or regulations by politicians that benefit the business interests of individuals who contribute money to the election of those politicians or lobby them after they are elected. Also, tyrannical societies can inhibit the personal incentives that drive personal achievement by confiscating too much of the financial rewards of the accomplishments of their citizens.

There is another more insidious pitfall for the individual member of any social order that is also very relevant to the theme of this book. It is the loss of the perception of the need for innovation and personal change. Societies provide specialized roles (e.g., family membership, jobs, professions, and so on) for their members. "Experts" to varying degrees have determined how one qualifies to effectively exercise these roles and carry out the processes that they entail. So, for those receiving, assimilating, and using this information, there may not be a clear-cut mandate to improve already-existing processes. One of the implied promises of joining an established group is that if the individual assumes a role and executes it according to the ways in which they were conceived, everything will be fine for him or her—not only in the present, but also into the future. Since we spend a lot of time in these activities, this can constitute a great deal of wasted opportunity for personal process improvement. In prehistoric times, the individual person existed more or less on his or her own without the modern social "safety nets". Innovation *on a personal level* was vital in order to make the best adaptations to shifting environmental forces. I believe that the notion that people are happier in smaller, simpler, less-specialized societies is at least partly derived from this dynamic. The individuals in those smaller, more "primitive" groups are less removed from challenges of their natural world environments. Therefore, he or she is forced to deal with the changing realities in their surroundings and the constant need to devise plans to avoid new threats or take advantage of new opportunities. Consequently, these people are more regularly engaged in vital personal process improvement activities. From an evolutionary point of view, it is logical that this kind of activity should be reinforced by positive feelings (i.e., happiness) since these activities are so closely linked to generational survival. As I mentioned above, in our more complex societies where new processes are devised by the relatively few, the mass dissemination of even very good ideas gives others an excuse not to exercise this valuable tool in the generation of personal fulfillment. I believe that if they did, they would experience happiness more often. This applies to persons in all strata of society. For example, it does not matter if you are a janitor or a cardiac surgeon, you have this wonderful opportunity. It does not matter if the "manual" you receive to do your work is one page long or thousands of pages long. It does not matter if the relevant "committee" deems that you have mastered the material in the manual and gives you a handsome certificate that documents adequate preparation for your job. You may still not be deriving as much fulfillment as possible from your life unless you are regularly reexamining the processes outlined in all of your "manuals" and instituting improvements on your own initiative, whenever feasible. That could be just re-reading it to relearn something you forgot about, amending it, or even re-writing it completely. That is because the essence of this *is a self-initiated improvement of the dimension of the person* who, for example, sweeps floors or transplants hearts.

This same kind of opportunity exists in virtually everything we do in life. These opportunities are more numerous than we generally think. In a later chapter, I will discuss how I saw this working in a broader range of the activities of daily life.

The Effect of the Expansion of Specialized Social Roles on Human History.

As discussed above, social organization provides significant survival advantages for the participating individuals. These include efficiencies in obtaining energy for their bodies, protection from environmental threats, and consequently, of course, increased odds for successful reproduction. In exchange, as technology advances, these individuals have to assume an ever-increasing number of specialized roles for the group. History has demonstrated that specialization is a double-edged sword. On one hand, it clearly fosters the advantages mentioned above, but on the other hand, some disadvantages as well. It can result in the relegation of individuals to classes that either restrict freedom or confer undue privileges, or even combinations of the two. Of course, in general, pursuits of efficiency in energy-gathering processes benefit those actively engaged in them as well as the rest of society. However, they can also trap individuals in both advantaged and disadvantaged social groups when societal forces conspire to keep them there. This could happen through laws that restrict class mobility (e.g. slavery) or when promises are made to grant groups of individuals economic benefits through a favored class status rather than through the personal execution of economic improvement strategies.

To understand this better, one can again look back to that hypothetical time, a *very* long time ago, when individuals, whose only ties were to their extended families, decided to associate with other individuals, outside their immediate families, into larger and larger groups.

Yuval Noah Harari, in his book, *Sapiens*, asserts that a genetic mutation which occurred between 70,000 and 30,000 years ago greatly facilitated this social change. The mutation led to improvements in language and other communication skills as well as the ability to function in larger groups through identification with abstract concepts such as gods, national symbols etc. This is called the "The Cognitive Revolution". It provided Homo sapiens such a profound survival advantage that it drove all other hominids, e.g. Homo neanderthalensis, out of existence.

These newly associating individuals might bring some special skill to the table, such as strength, speed, game tracking, tool making, hand-to-hand combat, or spiritual leadership. The individual, his or her family, and other members of the group would all benefit from these traits. However, there was no place to interview for a job with a corporation, sign up for a union, social security, Medicare or Medicaid, or unemployment insurance. Each partner in this transaction expects the other ones to deliver on their promised contributions. This expectation of commensurate rewards for one's work was reinforced by the positive feeling of "eating what you kill," (or, for any offended vegetarian, "reaping what you sow") that comes from the validation of any given individual's personal efforts. Everything happens with total transparency. If everyone pulls his or her weight and the group is better at environmental exploitation than its competitors, then the group thrives. If not, they need to contribute in other ways, move to compete elsewhere, or die.

In food acquisition for example, working in groups has clear-cut efficiency advantages compared with individuals working alone. Just compare the average gain in life-sustaining nutrition when you consider a single hunter catching a five-pound rabbit versus a group of a few dozen hunters killing an eighteen-thousand-pound wooly mammoth. Then factor in the boost of other fledgling industries that can be supported by the per-person gain in wealth: manufacturing of weapons, home construction, household goods, clothing, etc. Social organization can pay big dividends for the individual participants. (By the way, the modern-day equivalents of the designers of wooly mammoth hunts would be Henry Ford, Steve Jobs, Bill Gates, Mark Zuckerberg, Jeff Bezos.)

Consequences of the Cognitive Revolution were the Agricultural Revolution and much later the Industrial Revolution. About 10,000 years ago, agrarian societies emerged as their process changers made useful discoveries in the science of plant cultivation. Like cooperative hunting, agriculture provided new efficiencies in energy acquisition and became essential to the success of social groups who lived in areas of the world where this knowledge could be useful. However, as these things developed, specialization took an ugly, but arguably predictable turn.

In certain places, large, specialized groups of people emerged who worked the land largely for the benefit of small groups of ruling elites, supported by religious groups. In certain situations, the rulers were called gods, and in others, the clergy just asserted that a god or God had approved the arrangement (e.g., divine right). In exchange, these religious groups obtained protection, wealth, and power from the ruling elites and both entities persecuted those who were not on board with the arrangement. Consequently, the social structures that specialization spawned became suffocating to too many individuals, suppressing their freedom, thought, and initiative.

Jumping ahead in time, inspired by Enlightenment-era thinking, the United States was founded on principles that were a reaction to suffocating class systems, as well as to the dominant religious groups which were complicit in their maintenance. The founders of our nation were keenly aware of these issues. This is clearly reflected in the Constitution, which, in a large part, is comprised of rules that identify what rights are due to the individual and that also restrict centralized, governmental power. The American Revolution spurred the independence and democracy movements that have sprung up all over the world since then. How all this will end up is unclear. One somewhat-comforting take on this is that human beings had spent thousands of years devising social systems that, by their nature, repressed most of their individual participants. Only in the last few hundred years has the pendulum swung back toward a point where the success and happiness of the individual is a prime concern.

And that brings us back to the lessons I learned from dealing with excess dental plaque.

CHAPTER 9

APPLICATION TO OTHER LIFE ROLES

As I mentioned previously, I wanted to apply personal process improvement techniques to my other life roles, especially those connected with the greatest use of time (See Figure 3, Chapter 5). Making dental surfaces free of plaque and golfing occupy significantly less time than being a doctor, husband and father. And, beyond that, those latter three roles are much more complex when further analyzed for their sub-role components.

They also differ in that most of these sub-roles involve a relationship with another person.

This personal-relationship aspect poses the most significant challenge. There are plenty of laws, codes, and guidelines that describe, in general, how one should interact with another. However, there does not appear to be much information on how to employ strategies which make feelings of happiness or "spark(ing) of joy" a more likely byproduct of the activity. As I mentioned in the previous chapter, it is obvious that the individual life forms of many different species have found it beneficial to interact in a cooperative manner. More extensive sociological commitments depended on the recognition of the possibility that an association with another similar organism for a purpose other than just the production of a newborn could enhance survival of the individual participants and their offspring. As human societies have become more complex over time, individuals find themselves dealing with each other more and more, and yet may not really know how to make this a fulfilling experience. For many, relationships only exist as a trade-off to enhance survival. That is, they are behaviors guided by specific rules that, if followed, generally lead to a goal, and are not often regarded as opportunities for personal process improvement.

One could leave it that way and just live *through* those periods of time. However, since we spend so much time in those kinds of roles nowadays, it seems a shame to waste these numerous opportunities and let them remain as existential voids in our day.

This became clear to me one weekend when I was on call in our hospital. I had finished a procedure in the diagnostic imaging (X-ray) department and was conversing with one of the technicians who I knew casually through my numerous professional visits there. He introduced me to another technician who was there starting a temporary work assignment from an employment agency. I just exchanged greetings with that person and went back to my work. Later, I went down to the cafeteria for lunch. After I picked up and paid for my food, I walked out into the spacious dining area that was completely empty except for the DI technician on a temp assignment who I had met a couple of hours earlier. Ordinarily in that circumstance, I would have just waved hello, sat down by myself, quickly eaten my lunch, and gone back to work. However, by this time, I was already committed to the concept of deriving more from my personal interactions, and I asked the man if I could sit down with him. We had a conversation in which we eventually got to exchange views on what we considered to be the most important elements of our lives: our families, the meaning of our work, and so on. That lunch became one of the most personally fulfilling moments of the week.

The lesson for me here was to use these kinds of opportunities to enrich the experiences that societal life offers us.

As I go through these experiences, I believe they will support the goal of becoming a better doctor, husband, and father and that a feeling of happiness will result from the repeated attempts at making refinements in the processes which underlie their component roles.

In the next couple of chapters I will describe how I apply this strategy to my Doctor role, which currently requires the biggest investment of my time.

CHAPTER 10

LOOKING FOR PROCESS IMPROVEMENT OPPORTUNITIES AT WORK AND "WHY DO WE ALLOW OURSELVES TO SUFFER AT WORK AND WHAT CAN WE DO ABOUT IT?"

What follows here are examples of what one can do to identify personal renaissance opportunities in one's work day. I think this is very important since, by far, the greatest percentage of our waking hours is spent at work. The problem with the work day is that it is all too easy to take work activities for granted. We often tend to view them as just necessary expenditures of time for the sole purpose of acquiring the basic resources that promote the biologic success of ourselves and our loved ones, with the hope that there will be enough left over for some indulgences as well. This can lead to the unfortunate consequence of making work a time of indifference or even actual suffering that we voluntarily bear to enhance the biologic success of our families. Although this noble form of suffering lends the experience at least some degree of meaning, there is more to gain from the hours we devote to our jobs and professions. We will first need to drill down on the more specific components of our work roles. I will return to this issue of suffering later on in this chapter.

What I will describe below in my particular work situation has parallels in all lines of work.

When I finished training and first started to practice medicine, I thought that the majority of my time would be primarily spent gathering medical information about a patient's problem (through history taking, a physical examination, laboratory and diagnostic imaging tests, special procedures, etc.), and then telling patients what their problem was and what should be done about it. I have come to realize that assembling facts and arriving at diagnoses (depicted as the *"medical service provider"* in figure 7, below) are, in terms of time spent, relatively small components of what I do. To identify more specific roles under the general heading of my *"Doctor"* role, I made an analysis of the sub-roles that underlie the GI physician role at Puget Sound Gastroenterology ("PSG") just as I did for the golfer role in a previous chapter. See Figure 7, below.

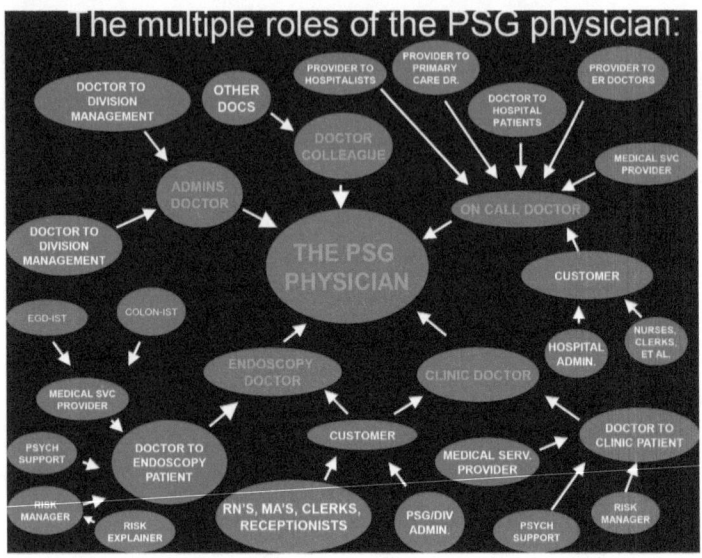

Figure 7

An understanding of all of the specific purposes of these roles is not important here. *What is more important is the fact that most of them involve personal relationships.* Consequently, most of the work day is spent relating in some way to another human being. Figure 7 turned out to be more complex than the one for "*the golfer*" for the obvious reason that being a doctor is more complicated than being a golfer. In any case, it still understates those complexities, as there are still many subcomponent roles not shown. These become more obvious as one looks for opportunities to experience a *personal renaissance*. It is not surprising that virtually all the physician roles involve relationships with other people, the exceptions being the specific activities of continuing medical education, information processing, and parts of the decision-making process.

Sometimes circumstances force us to more closely exam our roles in life. Remember the shame I experienced because of the failure to clean teeth properly? That was a one of those wake-up calls. Another occurred several years ago when I had an experience with a patient that made me seriously reexamine my role as *"risk manager"*, a sub-role of the doctor in the *"doctor to endoscopy patient"* relationship. I had identified potential problems in that area when I had a patient who experienced a recognized complication of a procedure that I had performed. The risk had been described to the patient in the consenting process before the procedure started. After an analysis of the event, I decided that I needed to improve the role of *"procedural risk explainer"*, a sub-role (shown in Figure 7) of the *"risk manager"* role. I devised what I thought were better ways to describe procedural risks. This involved steady eye contact and word choices that informed but did not scare the patient. One key element was to develop the skill to better establish whether or not the patient truly understood what was being explained. I learned through the use of good patient eye contact that people subtly reveal both doubt and lack of comprehension through their eyes. Improvements and utilization of this skill of *reading* the patient were very helpful in all of the other personal relationship roles encountered during the course of the day. As I implemented process-improvement strategies for my role as *"endoscopy risk explainer"*, I had the same experience I had as the Sonicare operator: a mini personal renaissance and then a continued feeling of fulfillment as I continue to refine this role—to this day.

Through attempts to improve my diverse, relationship-related roles, which I define as a *"doctor with a relationship to*

_____", I have fewer moments in which I feel that I am living *through time* and more moments in which I feel I am living *in time*. The result is experiencing fewer or less-pronounced existential voids. I have more moments when I am able to look back to the preceding few minutes and say to myself: "That was a meaningful and fulfilling experience."

In the first part of this chapter, I raised the issue of voluntary suffering at work. I suggested that too many people view their work more as an obligatory experience than a set of opportunities for personal transformation. I mentioned that we do this because of our natural sense of duty to provide for those close to us. Since what we receive in exchange for our labor is so vitally important to us and our families, we focus primarily on just the product of our work. In doing so, all too often we allow ourselves to see the activities of our work *just as a means to an end* and not as a series of opportunities to experience personal fulfillment. If, however, we *focus on the process rather than the outcome* (remember the Russell Wilson quotation), we can find opportunities for personal renaissances, however large or small they may be.

There are other factors that can make work a time of suffering to which all of us are prone and which are not necessarily attributable to self-sacrifice.

As an example of this, I will mention a specific job that doctors take on where the temptation to suffer is harder to resist. One of the major sub-roles that physicians have in our clinic is that of the on-call doctor. The on-call doctor takes all the hospital consultations and procedures as well as night call on a rotational basis, which leaves the more routine office duties to the rest of the physicians who are therefore freed from any work-related telephone calls at home. Many of us do not like to be the on-call doctor. I, myself, shared this opinion for some time. This is partly because it means we are working at nights and on weekends when we would rather be home with our families. But I believe some of this feeling comes from the stress of both coping with an unpredictable work flow and handling the heightened medical challenges of hospitalized patients who are more ill than the typical office patient. My theory is that, to some degree, each of us nobly bear on-call time as a necessary form of suffering for the sake of our colleagues.

But suffering creates problems. Others, who are closely involved in the process, such as the referring physicians (the emergency room doctors or the in-house internal medicine physicians), members of the hospital support staff, and what is even worse, *the patients themselves,* can be, from time to time, *subconsciously* identified by us as *agents contributing* to this suffering. This results in negative feelings toward these parties, which increase the level of suffering for everyone involved. The result of this can be a downward spiral of deepening unhappiness.

I know from conversations with patients that this can happen to people in all walks of life and in many different kinds of relationships, both at work and away from it.

Currently, although there are inevitable periods of real suffering (for example, the long days, and the occasional sleepless nights), I enjoy being the on-call doctor.

I believe the key to this enjoyment is the same as the key to having the most fulfilling experience you can in virtually any kind of relationship, whether at work or away from it. And therefore, the lesson applies to all other situations in which the sub-component role is a relationship with another individual. Essentially, the key is that one needs to recognize the other person as *self*, much like, as I mentioned in an earlier chapter, the cells that make up the immune system of a living organism need to recognize the cells of the other organs as *self* in order to avoid attacking them.

This point was illustrated in a movie that came out several years ago called *Philadelphia*. In this film, Tom Hanks plays a gay lawyer who is unfairly dismissed from his law firm while suffering from HIV/AIDS at a time before the availability of effective treatment for this deadly disease. As the movie nears its end, the main character is able to win his lawsuit against his previous associates with the help of another lawyer, a role played by Denzel Washington.

For me, the real story of this film was not how this legal victory was achieved. The real story was about the evolution of a deepening connection between the audience and Hanks' character.

In the beginning of the film, the character is shown in the balcony of a movie theater, engaging in sexual acts with random individuals. Later, he is seen as a slowly dying patient who has a stable, monogamous relationship with another person, played by the charismatic actor Antonio Banderas. Already the screenwriters have brought him closer to the film viewer by revealing his pitiful situation and then by showing his acceptance of a stable love relationship, a choice that would be approved by most of the film's viewers. However, the movie's central message is really driven home after the storyline has played out and Hanks's character has died. While the movie's credits are scrolling, the audience is shown what looks like a home movie of a little, curly-haired boy playing on the beach on a sunny, summer day. In other words, as the story played out, the viewers have been continually reminded of personal aspirations common to themselves and the main character—a desire not to suffer a fatal illness and the desire for the achievement of a stable loving relationship with another person. And finally, at the end of the film, the audience is left with the realization that Hanks's character could have been their son, brother, or grandchild. For the audience members, the most critical experience of the film is the ever-increasing connection they feel between themselves and him.

I think that the lesson here is that what really brings human beings together is the recognition of their mutual similarities rather than either a celebration or acceptance of their differences.

The application of this lesson to any relationship role is complicated by another issue. As I mentioned above, the on-call doctor has to reject the idea that he or she is a victim of the people with whom he or she is working. When one accepts this false notion, there is a tendency to justify the negative feelings with other, often erroneous or irrelevant judgments. For example, "Why is the ER doctor bothering me with this at this time? She must be stupid," or "God, if the patient weren't an alcoholic, he wouldn't be in this mess!" These observations help to legitimize the conclusion that one is being victimized but, of course, they exacerbate the suffering of all involved. However, once the referring doctor, and the support staff are identified as "self", everything falls into place. We accept the other parties as *self* when we acknowledge the obvious: that we all have a *common purpose*, in this case to take care of our shared patients in the best way possible.

Another step in improving a relationship involves a way of dealing with distinguishing features that may be perceived negatively, a point made in the opening scenes of

Philadelphia, when the main character is shown engaging in casual, self-destructive sexual activity. I believe this difficulty arises from the fact that we are programmed to use distinguishing features in situations of social conflict. Again, the biologic analogy is our immune system's recognition of *self* versus *non-self*. If the body "sees" an invading organism, such as a bacterium, as *non-self*, it will then attack it, kill it, and eliminate it from the host organism. The social equivalent of this was well illustrated in an old episode of *Star Trek* that featured Frank Gorsham. In that show, Gorsham played the roles of two stylized, twin characters who were dressed in full-body tights with hoods. Each suit was one-half black and one-half white. The scenes of the show were essentially sequential depictions of conflict between the characters without any obvious reason for their mutual animosity until the end of the episode. The characters reveal that they are enemies because, while one of them is wearing a suit with the black half on the *right* side, the other's black half is on the *left* side. This is an example of how recognition of differences can generate or sustain conflict through emotions and not reason. Of course, the specific message of this *Star Trek* show was to expose the stupidity of prejudice based on immutable physical characteristics, such as the color of one's skin.

But, in a more general sense, it shows how a perceived difference can be used as a tool to sustain conflict and, as a consequence, ultimately to sustain suffering. I believe that what is required to combat this is what I call the *objectification of perceived differences*. The first step for me is to identify in the other individual elements of current or past personal history that we have in common. I call this our "common core." I believe that the common core items have to be very specific for this process to work. It cannot simply be, for example, that we both are human beings, "God's children", etc. Common core items come from common past and on-going experiences, such as parenthood, being baseball fans, attending the same local high school, serving in the military, having to deal with a difficult child, traveling to the same place, protesting against the same thing, running a business, being a member of a union, thinking some unions are socially destructive, and many more. Once effective communication has provided the information to form this "common core," all the differences can be set aside as emotionally neutral observations (e.g., "She's gay, "He's Asian," "She's a drug addict," "He's young," She's old," "He's politically conservative," "She's an alcoholic," "He eats too much," "He's a Trump supporter, "She's a socialist", and so on).

In my profession, some of these set-aside issues cannot be ignored (e.g., "He's an alcoholic"). However, the experience for me as the physician and for the person who happens to have the serious problem of alcoholism can be improved significantly. In my mind, I picture that problem as sitting separately from the patient in a box, let's say, on the bedside table or a nearby chair. What are left for me within the space occupied by me and the patient are opportunities for personal connection. There is always something one can find. With this frame of reference, I can more effectively convey to the patient that alcoholism *does not define him or her as a person for me.* In fact, at times I actually use those very words. (By the way, when you are in this kind of situation, in any social context, you have to *really believe what you are saying*, you cannot lie. It won't work.) In essence, the alcohol problem has become a threatening object that is virtually separate from those elements that actually connect me with that person. Through this process of *objectification*, alcoholism simply has become something that we can attack in addition to all the medical issues that may or may not be related to it. We will not allow the existence of the condition to stigmatize the patient either for us or for that matter, for the patient him–or herself. This way, communication barriers come down, and important information can flow freely. This enhances the quality of medical decision making as well as the personal experience of the doctor and patient.

I have presented techniques that make interactions with another person a richer experience for me. Some of them, like the technique of *objectification of differences*, also should enhance the experience for the patient. What else could qualify as active strategies to make the experience better for the other person in the relationship?

I believe that the answer to that question lies in letting the other person know that you recognize their existence as a human being beyond the simple physical definition of flesh occupying space. Rene Descartes defined human existence in this way: "I think, therefore I am." This acknowledges that we of the species *Homo sapiens* are specifically distinguished from other living entities by the degree to which we can exercise our individual, uniquely powerful minds. When we are faced with the need to take advantage of environmental opportunities or to respond to perceived threats, there is the potential in each of us to gather information and use that information to formulate effective plans of action. I believe that there are not too many better ways to start a relationship than to acknowledge that the other party is a person fully capable of rational thought. There are good and bad ways to do that. Obviously, one does not shake hands and say "Hello. I'm _____. I honestly believe that you are fully capable of rational thought."

"Hollow" would not even begin to describe that.

The process I try to employ in is more complex. The first component is the manner in which I listen. I try very hard to let the patient speak without interruption. I listen as carefully as possible and maintain very close eye contact. I also ask them, if they do not spontaneously provide the information, what they think is wrong and what should be done about it. This conveys a very powerful message to the patient: I view them as a valuable contributor to the understanding and treatment of their illness by not only having gathered useful information about it but also by having interpreted the information in way that could lead to its successful resolution. That is, they have exercised their consciousness *at a high level,* that, not only defines them as a human being per se, but also as a better one at that. It is not so important whether their perceptions turn out to be correct or not. *It is important that you genuinely feel that they deserve consideration.* One helpful tool is to put yourself in a mindset such that you assume they *could be* correct until you have finished formulating your own thoughts toward the end of their visit. Faking interest is a very bad thing to do. Most people will pick up on this, and everyone hates to be patronized. In any case, I find that the patient's perceptions of the causes of their problems are not infrequently accurate.

(As an aside, I would say that the *physician* should make the *opposite assumption* about the accuracy of their own perceptions, that is: "I think the diagnosis is _____, but I could be wrong." This helps he or she to be open to alternative diagnoses and treatments as the case evolves.)

The technique, mentioned above, of letting the patient speak without interruption while taking his or her medical history is well-acknowledged as a means of being more effective physician, but is not often used enough. This is because doctors come with a very useful set of biases related to what we need to find out from their patients when they present with certain specific complaints. Current-day office visit times are getting shorter and shorter. Therefore, we will often attempt to dominate the conversation to get to that specific information. However, if we do not allow our patients or, for that matter, our customers, spouses, children, friends, colleagues, bosses, employees, or anyone else who we interact with significantly to fully present and establish their credentials as thinking human beings, we run a very high risk of making the time we spend in those relationships (which is a significant portion of our day) states of emptiness or even suffering.

When both parties in a social interaction are more satisfied with their experience in it, the more connected the parties become. The more connected they become, the more effectively they can exchange information, and the better the outcome of the interaction. If I perceive that I have brought about an improvement in the efficiency of these processes, I will then appreciate improvements in me personally as the operator of the processes involved. The result is another personal renaissance experience and a higher degree of happiness.

Setting personal improvement goals in this area is not all that difficult. Improvements can be made in techniques useful in seeking and finding shared characteristics. Through trial and error, I have discovered many of them. Again, the important thing is to believe that you are currently not as good at anything as you could be and to keep looking for ways to get better.

In personal interactions, outcome can generally be judged by feeling. I am not referring to the technical outcome of a medical consultation, such as "Did the bleeding stop?" or "Did the infection resolve?" Those are things that can be more or less objectively assessed by medical tools. The value of the of a personal interaction can be judged only subjectively. I try to tune in to an appreciation of the depth of feeling I experience right after it. For example, did this experience subjectively strike me as one that I would want to repeat? Did the patient seem to positively appreciate what happened? Did I feel these two outcomes were positively linked or mutually reinforced? Was there something about the way I felt that I would like to repeat in similar future situations? Did the time spent feel personally fulfilling?

I will use another example from my experience to illustrate how to retrospectively assess a patient interaction. To do this I will need to give two different versions of a medical consultation I provided a few years ago.

Version "A"

> The patient was admitted to the hospital with the complaint of blood in the stool. I was called in to evaluate this new symptom. A flexible endoscope was passed in the lower intestine and I found a bleeding growth. A biopsy was made. The biopsy showed cancer. I called the surgeon, and the growth was removed.

Version "B"

The patient was admitted to the hospital with the complaint of blood in the stool. I was called in to evaluate the new symptom. He was a middle-aged, male (like me!) software engineer (okay, not me) who has three grown children (just like me!). I noted that the patient had previous surgery to remove a cancerous tumor from the lower bowel, which required the placement of a colostomy—that is, an attachment of the lower bowel to the skin of the abdomen so that stool can flow out into a bag attached to the opening of the bowel on the skin. The patient had several other past and chronic medical conditions. One of these was the amputation of his left leg to treat a *different* cancerous growth. A flexible endoscope was passed in the lower intestine, and a bleeding growth was found and biopsied. I discussed the finding with the patient and his family. The family had significant anxiety related to the possibility that the growth could be a recurrence of the previously treated bowel cancer. I discussed the potential therapeutic strategies with them in detail. When I read the pathology report that the growth was indeed a recurrent cancer, tears came to my eyes. I called the surgeon, and the growth was removed.

In versions "A" and "B," we can find the same technical process that solved the clinical problem posed by the presenting symptom, rectal bleeding. The difference, of course, is the depth of the personal connection between me and the patient. This depth was created by my awareness of shared core elements such as age, sex, and family characteristics. It was fueled by the recognition of the other person's previous suffering and understandable current fears. The depth of our connection was reflected in my emotional reaction to the reality of the nature of the growth as reflected by the pathology report.

For me, the meaning of the interaction was increased by both the success of the technical result as well as the depth of the doctor–patient personal connection. Therefore, the added value to me of investing effort in the process of personal connection was the increase in the meaning of a relatively small, but important segment of my time on earth. This was time I would have spent anyway because of my commitment to perform gastroenterology consultations when requested. To be able to receive this added valve required refinements in my role as a "*doctor with a relationship to a patient*". These refinements led to personally perceived improvements in my skill in this role. And this increase in skill level indicated to me that there has been a rebirth of the elements of myself that perform the role.

Does this occur in every patient interaction that I have? Of course not. I am a human being, prone to failure in all of my endeavors. Do I shoot par or better on any of my rounds of golf? No, I don't.

Although a better answer to that question would have been: "*No, not yet*".

CHAPTER 11

MONEY AND POSSESSIONS

You can't write a book about happiness without commenting on money. Many things have been said about money, such as "Money makes the world go 'round"; "Money can't buy me love"; "Money can't buy you happiness"; "Money don't get everything, it's true, but what it don't get, I can't use! Gimme moooooooney…that's what I want!"; and "… the love of money is the root of all evil". But what is money in reality and what role does it play in the pursuit of happiness?

As mentioned in a previous chapter, money is a device created by society to facilitate the exchange of goods and services among its members. So, in general, one receives money in exchange for whatever one produces, in a quantity that theoretically represents the value that society, through its many, diverse markets, assigns to the work that produces the goods or service in question.

So, how does that relate to finding happiness?

For most of us who do not live directly off the land, so to speak, money is required to obtain fuel for our bodies and for the bodies of our loved ones. So, to some degree, it is directly related to the prime goal of all living things—successful, repetitive reproduction. Therefore, the activity that produces the amount of money that a given person feels is necessary to nurture and protect his or her own body and the bodies of his or her offspring will carry a great deal of meaning for that person. And so, based on the theories I present in this book, improvements in the processes that make up all of those activities should generate happiness. When you consider the costs of education, food, shelter, healthcare, and other living expenses, and throw in the costs of personal indulgences, the resultant dollar number could be quite high but will vary from person to person. That point was illustrated by a television ad campaign from a few years for a large investment company that asks you "What's your number?" The commercial shows a bunch of otherwise sane-looking adults walking about, carrying large signs with dollar figures that vary from several hundred thousand to a few million. These are supposed to represent their individual conclusions about how much money they need for a happy retirement.

A great deal of the variability of "your number" stems from personal differences in the specifics of what we purchase, especially when it comes to indulgences. After all, there are a lot of fairly expensive items to choose from: sleek, fast cars of high status symbol value; a closet full of shoes; season tickets to the ballet or opera; movies; expensive restaurants; pleasure boats; ATVs; that cabin on the lake, at the shore or in the mountains; sporting events; golf club memberships; chocolate cake; alcohol; cocaine; and so on.

Let me emphasize again that these activities are fine, except for the cocaine, as long as we have the extra resources for them and partake of them in the appropriate quantities and contexts. As I mentioned in a previous chapter, I find it useful to separate them into activities which just result in pleasurable sensory experiences from those that support improvements in processes under our personal control. For example, eating chocolate cake results in a pleasant sensory experience that lasts for a few seconds after each bite and does not require any special skill. Watching a play or movie could just provide us a short-lived, pleasant emotional experience or perhaps a momentary escape from an otherwise stressful day. On the other hand, the story, at least in certain cases, could also teach us something that could spawn a positive change in one of our personal roles. A trip to the cabin could afford one some well needed rest, increased physical activities and could also create an atmosphere that fosters creative thinking. Which of these activities holds the most promise for generating *an enduring* sense of fulfillment? How would you apportion your extra monetary resources among these types of experiences?

Now I will turn back to the issue of the value of money *per se*. It is useful to think of amounts of money as points in a scoring system for the activities that generate it. If, for example, you operate a business that generated x number of dollars one year and the next year it generated $2x$, then one could say that your operation of the processes that governed that profit increase had significantly improved. This could support a personal renaissance experience that comes with the perception of having improved as an operator of those processes.

Beyond that, the mere *possession* of money really lacks meaning. What does it mean once you have the resources to feed yourself and your dependent loved ones, to educate them, and to prepare for future needs for nourishment, shelter, and some reasonable self-indulgences along the way? It would have the same meaning as the 250th soup spoon acquired by a hoarder and put away in a drawer never to be used. The object itself does not serve any function except as a marker of a neurotic act.

Money needs to have a life after acquisition. It cannot just be a trophy. Trophies themselves do not engender happiness. They are just the *consequence of the actions that went into acquiring them*. The sense of fulfillment experienced by the person now in possession of the trophy actually came from becoming the person who eventually earned it.

I believe that this is where a person has the opportunity to pursue the goal of spiritual immortality. Virtually all religions and many non-religious philosophies share a belief in the *existence of the soul*, that is, a non-physical, but enduring element within all of us. And that the soul is on a *journey*, the success of which depends on how we act during the course of our natural lives. An example of this is the belief shared by Jews, Christians, and Muslims that a person's performance of good deeds during his or her time on earth will result in their soul's successful journey back to God, whether during life or after life ends or both. Even if this is not your belief, helping others is on most people's list of the roles that define them as good people. (See the next chapter.) Giving away some portion of your retained wealth in a thoughtful, *personal*, and constructive manner is another way to practice personal process improvement and have personal renaissance experiences.

One of the best examples of how to go about this was contained in a sermon I heard on charitable giving in which our priest described the upbringing of a philanthropist he knew from his work in another Parish. This man grew up during the depression of the 1930's, in what was the most economically devastated region of the country, the dust bowl of Oklahoma. His family was so poor they did not have the resources to move to California which is what many local families did in that era to escape poverty. In order for his family to survive, every member, including the children, had to work. So, the philanthropist, then a young boy, brought in a regular income, although, in those days, the kind of work he could get could only render about ten cents per day. The key part of this story is that his mother gave him very specific instructions on what to do with each dime he brought home. There were three old coffee cans on the counter in their tiny kitchen. The first was labeled "share", the second one was labeled "save" and the third, "spend". The first dime he brought home went into the "share" can, the second dime went into the "save" can, and the third into the "spend" can. When he grew up, he became extremely wealthy in the oil and natural gas exploration business. (That is, he went on several, *very* successful "wooly mammoth hunts"!) Throughout his life, he has continued that same pattern of sharing, saving, and spending, *with sharing coming first*, that he learned from his mother when he and his family had very little money. By all accounts, he has remained a very happy, spiritually fulfilled person ever since he put that first dime in that old coffee can labeled "share".

CHAPTER 12

CITIZENSHIP AND MORALITY

In the course of *social* evolution, many different "social organisms" have emerged. Our participation in these groups helps to define who we are in many ways. We spend significant amounts of time as members of them. How we utilize these particular units of time can become important for us in terms of the levels of self-fulfillment that we can experience. How do we approach this situation in a way that allows us to exercise the elements of personal process improvement?

This becomes clearer if we look at our affiliations in a certain way.

If one recognizes that he or she is a parent, an iron worker, a union member, a fascist, a Christian, a U.S. citizen, a student, CEO of a large corporation, a janitor, a dog owner, a tennis player, a communist, and so on, at some point they will have filed away a mental list of what constitutes being in that role. For example, the U.S. citizen would have a list entitled "*U.S. Citizen*," and underneath that title would be the characteristics that person accepts to qualify him or her to be included in that group of people. In this case, the elements would be something like "born within the borders of the United States of America" or "born elsewhere but successfully completed the legal requirements for citizenship in the United States of America." The list for a father would have the heading "Father," and under that could be "participated in the conception of a human being by providing sperm" but also could have "adopted a child" on that list. It just depends on that person's unique situation.

We really cannot grow in any sense until we have a concept of who we are. We are all more multi-dimensional than we think. And we cannot really know who we are until we examine ourselves for the roles that are associated with each of those dimensions. And only then are we ready to identify the elements that qualify us as legitimate actors in those roles.

The next key element of this is that we attach a specific word to the title of each list in question for us. This word is the adjective, *good*. Now, the items that define the role at the top of the list lead us more directly to specific process changes that can result in personal renaissance experiences.

So now, the list that, for example, is entitled "*Good U.S. Citizen*" is going to become more complex and, therefore, more interesting. The elements on this list will most often come from other individuals, but they will be adopted as reasonable by the person who bears the list in his or her consciousness. For example, one could have "votes in an informed manner in every election" or "supports the military"; or another might put "supports efforts to provide healthcare to every citizen" or even "supports efforts to secure the borders." Beneath each of these entries would be more specific roles that would be obviously amenable to process improvement efforts. Here is a partial example of this with parts of the thinking process in parentheses:

(I am a) ***Good U.S. citizen*** (because I...)

- **Vote in an informed manner in every election by...**
    - Reading the voters' pamphlets
    - Reading newspaper articles and editorials
    - Watching candidate debates
    - Debating people with other points of view
    - Filling out the ballot or visiting the polls on time

- **Support the military by...**
    - Serving in the military
    - Having served in the military
    - Contributing to Veterans' welfare by...
        - Giving donations to a Veterans' charity
    - Saying "thank you" to veterans I meet

So, if one accepts the above, by simply reading the pamphlets, newspaper articles, and editorials, or by watching the debates, discussing the issues with others, and completing the process by actually voting on time, one has fulfilled the elements that qualify him- or herself as an informed voter which, in turn, supports the notion that he or she is a good U.S. citizen.

Is that enough? No. I think there is more here. Instead of just settling for the adjective "*good*", let's try "*better*". The effect of that is that it promotes the seeking of ways to perform the supporting roles better. This means that you must more specifically address the processes involved. For example, take the process of reading a voters' pamphlet. Do we just read the opinion we tend to favor, or do we read the opposing point of view? Did we do our best to reconcile the contrasting points of view? Maybe we could devise a new process to accomplish this goal in a more efficient manner. If we do all of that and believe that we arrived at a better decision regarding a specific voting issue, then we have become a *better voter* and therefore a *better U.S. citizen*; and because citizenship is clearly an important role for us, the end result is that we have become *better people*. In that way it becomes a personal renaissance experience.

Our concepts of what is moral, just, right, and correct are obviously important elements in the production of these "lists." Generally, the concepts are passed on to us from others, (e.g., parents, teachers, philosophers, newspapers, a member of the clergy, the Constitution, novels, friends, television opinion shows, and so on) but also could be our own creations. Wherever they come from, if we truly accept them, they will provide the meaning for the processes that support living them and, in turn, the activity to improve those processes which makes us reborn in our role as a "*Citizen*".

CHAPTER 13

THE INEVITABILITY OF INTER-GROUP CONFLICT

Presumably, most people would consider living together in harmony to be a desired goal. If that is so, then why do we fight with each other so much?

When we talk about inter-group conflict of any type or scale, except for the purely symbolic ones, such as some sporting events, we could include war and terrorism, racial and ethnic strife, political campaigns, competition for a market by businesses, competition by a union with other unions to represent a group of workers or with businesses over worker compensation, and so on.

What is the basic issue?

I believe the genesis of conflict is rooted in the basic biological imperative, that is, the seeking of physical immortality, combined with the perception of a limited supply of or access to energy and other environmental resources. As I mentioned before, seeking physical immortality requires the acquisition of sources of energy to run the biologic organism giving it a chance to reproduce before the natural deterioration of the organism's physical structure occurs, or before some outside force ends its existence.

The perception of limited access to energy resources can be viewed as follows. (I am updating this based on current knowledge of the world, but I think it has worked throughout history in some analogous form.) The earth is basically a big ball. We cannot live buried under its surface or at an altitude greater than roughly twenty thousand feet above its sea level. Most life forms exist in a space occupied by a relatively thin layer of gases and in the ocean where all life originated in the first place. This space is finite. There are practical limits to anyone's ability to exploit existing resources, and it is unlikely that we all will soon be able to jump on spaceships and move to another planet. I am sure that ancient people looked at their immediate environments and did not think that they could address this issue *only* by moving great distances elsewhere. By and large, the most practical option was to out-compete their neighbors. This would quite often involve hostile confrontations. An explicitly stated, 20th century example of this was one of Hitler's justifications for war on his neighbors in Europe: the acquisition of "lebensraum" which is German for "living space".

The next important factor that I have not discussed relates to the fact that although we may aspire to love one another, it is impossible for a given individual to love or treat everyone else *equally*. We all have priorities in this regard. For example, we will put our close family members before others in our neighborhoods. We will generally put people in our own social groups ahead of those in other social groups.

If you do not think this is true, imagine the following scenario, especially if you have ever had a child: You are walking along the edge of a cliff holding the hand of your twelve-year-old daughter on one side and the hand of her best friend on the other. (I know, you are smart enough not to do this, but that does not matter to illustrate this point.) Suddenly, the earth underneath both of the girls gives way, and the kids slip over the edge of the cliff, dangling over jagged rocks a thousand feet below. You are trying your best to hang on to both of them, but you do not have the strength to keep each child's hand from slipping slowly out of your grip. Your options are: (1) To lose both of them; (2) Release the friend and put all your effort into saving your child; (3) Release your child and put all of your effort into saving the friend; or (4) Fall off the cliff with the two of them. Answer honestly. Which of these actions would you choose? Or, if you prefer to consider a less gloomy scenario, how often does it happen that a neighbor knocks on your door and offers to pay for your kid's college tuition? This kind of hierarchy of attachment applies to inter-group dynamics as well. We tend to favor our children over other children and the members of our groups over the members of other competing groups.

Now, add in the nagging worry about which group will win the competitive game of energy acquisition, and I think you will find the basis for inter-group conflict that is so evident throughout our history. Bickering over cultural or racial differences is just a tool that social groups use to create their own group identities and to sustain some kind of emotional state (usually hate) that supports aggressive actions against the competing group. In my analogy to the biologic organism, I called this the recognition of *self (us)* versus *non-self (them)*. Once the immune system of a multicellular organism recognizes some other organism as *non-self*, it will launch an attack against it, "killing" it or driving it out of the organism. In the social realm, it is hard to fight a war where people may have to risk their lives while trying to take the lives of others, without the compelling force of hate for the individuals they will need to kill. It helps justify the action they have to take. To a lesser degree, in other types of conflicts, for example in political battles, it helps to motivate the members of a political party if they can characterize the opponent party members as mean, stupid, racist, privileged, out of touch with reality, or warmongers. That is, "they are certainly not as good as we are". In wars between nations, territories and natural resources are gained. In politics, it is power that is at stake, which translates into money, and money gives the winners greater access to life-sustaining resources, which is what at least some of the most ardent members of the group wanted when they joined in the first place.

Yes, it is true that for 46 years after World War II, the world avoided massive conflict between the super powers (the United States, Western Europe and their economically aligned allies versus the Soviet Union and their client states) because of the deterrent of mutually assured destruction. However, diverse groups, each held together by their own specific national, ethnic or religious characteristics, have taken their own independent paths of self interest in Asia, Africa, Eastern Europe, and the Middle East. This has led to local traditional wars, terrorism, and even horrendous examples of genocide. And, unfortunately, this pattern will likely continue. International trade creates economic interdependency that should help prevent conflicts between the nations involved. However, there are always going to be arguments over what is fair trade and there will always be some parties who feel that they have been left out.

As a physician, I look at this situation like *most* of the problems we have to deal with in medical practice. There are a few diseases that can be cured (for example: acute appendicitis, peptic ulcer disease, specific types of pneumonia, some types of cancer), but there are many more that cannot be cured and need to be *managed*. Those diseases, e.g. coronary artery disease, inflammatory bowel disease, arthritis, the irritable bowel syndrome, emphysema, will always plague us to some degree or another. We, as doctors, nurses, medical research scientists, medical product developers, etc., have to do what we can to mitigate the adverse effects of these illnesses for our patients.

The conditions which I outlined in the first part of this chapter, that underlie conflict between groups of human beings, will not change. There will always be friction between groups of people as they compete for the environmental resources. At the level of international conflict, one can only hope that our national leaders can come up with effective plans for mitigation against the potential damage that can occur as we address the external threats that face our country.

CHAPTER 14

SPIRITUALITY, HAPPINESS, AND PERSONAL PROCESS IMPROVEMENT

In essence, this book represents my attempt to explain how to live in a way that engenders feelings of happiness. Maximizing time spent doing things that have meaning for the individual seeking happiness is a key element. I have put forth the idea that because we are living entities, we are compelled to pursue a basic biologic purpose: the pursuit of physical immortality. This goal, so deeply engrained in all of us, confers meaning to many of the roles we play in our daily lives. So, for example, we work to acquire the money to pay for nourishment and protection of ourselves and our families, as well as the preparation of our sons and daughters to carry on after us. The overall significance of that goal should inspire attempts to make ourselves better at the specific personal processes that lead to its achievement. But all too often that does not happen. We tend to take for granted that at the end of the pay period, the money will be there if we can just get through the minutes, hours, and days in between. Units of time at work begin to lose their intrinsic meaning and then become the existential voids I described in an earlier chapter. This situation is salvaged when an appreciation of the importance of the outcome of the work drives us to focus on making improvements in the underlying processes that generate the outcome. This positive transformation of process allows the perception of the positive transformation of self, i.e., the *personal renaissance experience.*

However, even if we are rewarded by feelings of fulfillment as we pursue physical immortality, we all must face a series of disappointments. Our children grow up and leave our homes, diminishing one of our primary reasons for biologic existence—our role as parents. Our bodies begin a long, initially slow, but steady decline in functional capacity after our late twenties. Accidents of all kinds happen. We make bad choices. Our zealous pursuits of sensory stimulation leave us empty all too soon. Even the people who love us the most will sometimes fail us in some way. Our lives pass in the blink of an eye and end, for many, in a too-slow, downward slide toward death. While the *pursuit of physical immortality* may be a good plan for our DNA and for us while we are alive and reasonably functional, at the end of our physical existence we, as we knew ourselves, are no longer around to execute it. And even before we reach that point, along the way, our bad luck and bad choices can lead to the conclusion that physical existence no longer has enough meaning for us. At these moments the appreciation of the meaning of existence will require varying degrees of mental gymnastics, a set of skills that we all should find worthwhile developing.

Let me explain this idea with a personal story. I am a member of an Episcopal Church. However, from as far back as I can remember our family attended a Congregational church, a relatively "liberal" protestant denomination, where I served as an altar boy. After becoming a teenager, I had very little contact with any church at all until I had an epiphany about 10 years ago which led me to my current spiritual home.

However, to my great surprise, just after graduating from high school, my parents told me something about our family's past that they had never mentioned before. I had known that I was born a few weeks after my mother arrived in the United States with my sister from post-World War II Romania. My father came a few months later. What I found out at this time was that my parents and most of my extended family were Jewish. Some had survived the Holocaust and many did not. My mother, Madeleine, and her family were taken to Auschwitz in 1944. This included both of her parents, a married sister, Gabriella, and another married sister Clara and her children. Gabriella's and Clara's husbands along with my mother's two brothers were forced into slave labor with the German forces on the Russian front. Upon their arrival at Auschwitz, Clara, her children were murdered in a gas chamber. Not too long after that both of her parents were killed. The bodies were burned in a mass bonfire as the Nazi extermination schedule had sped up to a point that exceeded the functional capacities of the cremation ovens. One of Madeleine's brothers was the only man in the family to come back from the Russian front. Madeleine and her sister Gabriella were spared the fate of the other family members and worked as slave laborers in the concentration camp. They did not share the same barracks but would occasionally see each other and talk. At one of these meetings, Gabriella said something to the effect: "I believe that God put us here so that we can understand what our husbands are going through at the front lines." My mother replied to her younger sister, "We all must be strong."

The significance of that latter statement relates to something I have yet to mention. You see, when the soldiers came to my grandparents' home to take the family to what amounted to a cattle train to Auschwitz, everyone was lined up and counted. Missing from the line was the skinny, little 7-year-old girl named Marta who would become my older half-sister. My mother Madeleine did something that virtually no Jewish mother in the area did at the time. She hid her only child with a local Christian family and paid them with cash that was sewn into the cushion of a chair. She convinced the officer in charge that her daughter was elsewhere.

And that is how my mother and sister survived World War II.

My sister, Marta, survived because my mother kept her out of Auschwitz where, at least by that time, young children were immediately exterminated. My mother survived for two reasons. The first was that she did not have a child with her. Mothers were needed to keep their children calm as they were herded into the gas chambers for the alleged "shower".

The second reason is the point behind bringing all this up. She had to be "strong" for a reason. She needed to survive the unspeakable Hell of where she was and get back home to raise the little child she left behind. The pursuit of this goal provided her the meaning for her incarceration in the concentration camp and helped her get through each terrifying moment of her stay. Gabriella's statement was also an attempt to assign meaning to her situation through the assertion that it was in God's plan for her to endure this suffering so that she could understand the suffering of her husband. Unfortunately, while Madeleine and Gabriella both made it out of Auschwitz, only my mother made it all the way home. Home to her little daughter, Marta.

Gabriella's observation of God's role in her tragic predicament introduces the idea of a role for spirituality in our lives. In my opinion, in order to experience the spiritual realm, one must *defer to a power beyond us*. I call that power God, but others can use a different term or not name it if they wish. In an effort to diffuse the "name" issue, let me describe that power as a *consciousness that transcends our own mortal consciousness*. Let's call it the "*Transcendent Consciousness*". The *Transcendent Consciousness* possesses a depth and breadth of awareness incomprehensible to us woefully ignorant and flawed Homo sapiens, denizens of the surface of what amounts to a speck of dust in the universe, apparently one of many. Yes, we are lucky enough to possess a mutation in our DNA that allows us to learn from observations of our surroundings and translate that learning into effective actions that give us the upper hand on the rest of the living creatures of our relatively isolated, tiny world. However, scientists will tell you that whenever we learn any fact in any scientific field, ten more questions come up that beg for answers. We will never have all the answers.

Although what we do know has provided us with all the amazing advancements of science and technology, those advancements do have an untoward effect on the individual's sense of self-worth. I remember the time when, with a little training or reference to a manual, a person could service their own automobile. Cars have become so complex that self-servicing of cars is not really feasible anymore. Ask yourself this question: "Is there any one individual who could create a cellphone from the component raw materials?" I doubt it. Our personal functional limitations require the use of teams (specialized social organisms) to accomplish complex technological tasks. Essentially, we are depending on the competence of the team's *shared* consciousness. But even then, the team that, for example, makes sequential iterations of the cell phone will always fail to make the perfect one since new technical discoveries will eventually make the current version inadequate in some way. And there is no end to the discoverable knowledge in the cell phone-relevant sciences. So, in the modern world, we, as individuals, increasingly find ourselves diminished, less able to do the big things on our own. Even worse, we can end up being replaced by the machines that we have created. Where does that leave us? It leaves us facing the limitations of our own consciousnesses.

But what if we are able to defer to the *Transcendent Consciousness*, an entity that understands all that we have not yet understood as well as all that which we will never be able to understand; an entity that has been, is, and will be the ultimate creative force in nature and in the supernatural? That deference opens us to one of the most wonderful gifts one can ever receive. The gift is the realization that while perfection exists in the *Transcendent Consciousness*, it cannot exist in mortal consciousness, both individual and collective. This allows us to set down the burden that comes with pretending we are perfect or that we are even capable of perfection. In essence, we are excused from having to solve every problem we face. I cannot tell you how often I see patients whose symptoms are related to anxiety caused by an inability to shrug off the responsibility for solving problems over which they have no control.

Think of how many times you have heard an elite athlete, when interviewed after a victory, credit God for his or her performance. Many people chafe at this kind of statement because they assume that the athlete is asserting that God was on their side in the just completed contest. I do not think that is usually the intention of the statement. I would translate the usual post-game interview catch phrase of "All (the) glory (goes) to God" as the following: *"The talents of me, my teammates and coaches are gifts from the Transcendent Consciousness whose dimensions defy definition. Though we are basically flawed, we used them in an effective way. All credit goes to the Transcendent Consciousness!"* And if the same person were interviewed after a defeat, he or she would say: *"The use of the gifts which proceed from Transcendent Consciousness favored the flawed human beings on the other team. The outcome of this athletic contest is a message from the Transcendent Consciousness. That message is that we, being also inherently flawed, have to better utilize the gifts of talent that we have received"*. This deference to an all-knowing, all powerful force, well beyond our capacity of understanding, is the key to the avoidance of the anxiety associated with the inevitable failures that we all experience. This focus on the "better utilization of gifts of talent" also increases the meaning of the personal process improvement strategies that make athletes better athletes and results in the experience of a sense of fulfillment while they are being employed in training.

Okay, so all of this requires *a belief in the existence* of a *Transcendent Consciousness*. Belief could be just blind faith but is best supported by some kind of communication. This could occur in a church, synagogue, mosque, or a temple. It could be accomplished through prayer or meditation anywhere or anytime. It could even happen in a dream. An appreciation of the *Transcendent Consciousness* cannot be achieved with the scientific tools we use to understand the physical world. It is a different kind of *knowing*. In my mind it is more akin to the feeling that we have when we connect with another person, similar to the experience I described in a previous chapter with the patient who had the bleeding colon cancer. Even people who do not believe in God describe spiritual experiences in the course of relaxation exercises or meditation. Could these events be examples of connection with the *Transcendent Consciousness*? Regardless of how they come about, these experiences can and, in my opinion, should be a positive, fulfilling sensation. Why? Because this link between our individual consciousnesses and the omniscient, omnipresent, and omnipotent *Transcendent Consciousness* brings us closer to the goal of existence in the spiritual realm. A place where there is the promise of a life denied us during our mortal existence on Earth, a life that is truly ever-lasting.

In any case, I believe that, given the nature of our earthly existence, even if we did not believe in a *Transcendent Consciousness*, at some point in our lives, we would surely benefit from conjuring one up.

Religions are social organisms that, like their constituent, human organisms, have their own flaws, but also can help anyone make that spiritual connection. Although the formal details of the various ceremonies differ from faith to faith, they all are designed to facilitate that effect. The religions I know also offer direct guidance toward the renaissance experience that I keep referring to when I discuss *personal process improvement*. While one may continue to sin, one still has the chance to be forgiven and try to make oneself better. There are the born-again Christian groups. But many other religious groups also provide this opportunity in some form on almost any visit to their houses of worship. Religions define clear standards of conduct that populate our "I am a good _____ because..." lists and serve as goals for personal improvement strategies. Participants are judged by these standards. When they do not measure up, they generally can, by the grace of the *Transcendent Consciousness*, be forgiven if they are willing to change directions. Then they have the opportunity to improve and be reborn as new, better versions of their former selves. While there may be a promise of everlasting life down the road, this feeling of personal rebirth is as undeniable as it is powerful.

Our journey to spiritual immortality must begin with the acknowledgment of a level of consciousness infinitely greater that our individual consciousnesses and the collective consciousness of our species. It allows us the refuge of not having to be perfect, or right all the time, and to not take ourselves to too seriously. (What peace that refuge can provide!) That acknowledgement may steer us to places that afford us communion with that superior consciousness (the "*Transcendent Consciousness*" presented above). Those places could include a quiet space like anywhere with one's eyes closed or a physical structure where people gather who have accepted a set of specific concepts regarding the nature of this superior consciousness. These concepts could also include the group's interpretations of the superior consciousness's instructions regarding optimal human behavior that could guide anyone in their own personal process improvement endeavors.

Ultimately this deference to the *Transcendent Consciousness* brings closer to a union with that all-powerful, everlasting force and the pursuit of spiritual immortality, *fulfilled*.

CHAPTER 15

SUMMARY

I believe that we all have the opportunity to experience happiness when we chose to live life in a certain way.

So then, what is "Life"?

Life, in the biologic sense, is essentially a journey in which we are compelled to pursue a path towards a goal that we share with all living things, no matter how great or small: the preservation of our own unique, individual physical identities (encoded in DNA) though the time of our existence in the natural world and then, well beyond that in the modified forms that constitute our offspring. I have labeled this journey "*the pursuit of physical immortality*".

Life, in the spiritual sense, is pursued through connections we make with a *supernatural* consciousness, whose dimensions defy human comprehension. I have called this the "*Transcendent Consciousness*". Actions in this arena bring us toward the preservation of our unique spiritual identities through time beyond our time as well. I have labeled this journey "*the pursuit of spiritual immortality*".

In the pursuit of these two goals we find ourselves acting in various roles which vary in complexity. The levels of their complexities are proportional to the number of sub-roles associated with them. My thesis is that if we can improve ourselves as actors in these roles, we will be rewarded with the experience of happiness. This emotional reward exists to reinforce personal improvement activities which are critical elements of the overall goal of increasing the odds of both biologic success (the path toward "physical immortality") as well as spiritual success (the path to an everlasting connection with a consciousness that transcends our own consciousnesses).

In order to find opportunities for these personal improvement efforts we need to know as much as possible about the roles we play in our lives. This means that we will need to examine them very carefully and identify their most basic components. A basic component role is, in essence, one in which a *very specific element of ourselves* controls a *very specific process*. Focusing on more basic roles leads to more satisfying results from personal improvement strategies. I introduced this concept by identifying the sub-role of "The Sonicare Operator" which supported the more general role of "The Teeth Cleaner". (The role of "Teeth Cleaner" has multiple components). The problem identified was in the use of the Sonicare device. So, the role of the "the Sonicare Operator" got the attention of the process improvement plan. Another benefit of this kind of focus is the mitigation of shame. We know that we are all flawed, but complex, multi-dimensional creatures. So, having a deficiency in one area does not diminish the possibility of doing quite well in others. The result of this is the well-deserved preservation of self-esteem!

There are three other considerations that need to be kept in mind when we choose to focus attention on any role. One is the need to choose roles whose outcomes we have control over. Too much anxiety results from assuming we can fix all of the problems we face in life, let alone problems over which we have no control. The second consideration is to focus on roles in which we spend greater amounts of time. And the third relates to the level of meaning the role holds for us. The degree of happiness we can expect to experience addressing a role (and consequently its sub-roles) will vary directly with the amount of meaning we assign to it. I illustrated that point in my description of my visit to the new dental office. The process behind teeth cleaning suddenly acquired meaning when the new dental hygienist examined my teeth and essentially asked me if I was caring for them at all. More specifically, meaning was created by the shame I experienced in that moment. I also provided the example of how my mother, Madeleine, mentally framed the meaning of her presence in a Nazi death camp as a challenge to exercise her will to survive and get home to her young daughter, Marta. And how her sister, Gabriella, attached meaning to her experience there through her belief that God had created her situation so that she could understand the suffering of her husband.

Roles that either directly or indirectly lead to the successful acquisition of energy or successfully preparing offspring for life, as well as those that potentially enhance the survival potential of the individual's social groups inherently have significant meaning. Role support sensory experiences (e.g. eating and sexual activity) have much less meaning when exercised solely for their pleasure-producing properties. Instead they produce fleeting moments of pleasant sensory stimulation; and when partaken in excessive quantities and in the wrong contexts can ultimately be damaging.

The meaning of the pursuit of spiritual immortality lies in the recognition of the inherent limitations of our physical existence. We are able to continue to exist after our deaths, at least in a certain sense, by passing on genetic information to succeeding generations of offspring. On the other hand, *spiritual immortality* promises the eternal preservation of a defining element of us which transcends our physical identities.

The recognition of the fact that both sets of opportunities exist for us is very important but does us no good unless we take advantage of them.

To be able to take advantage of these opportunities, we must see ourselves as actors in an *ever-present now*. We need to avoid living as prisoners of our pasts. This means that we should look to the past only for lessons that help us make better choices in our present. We should not let the past define us or set limits for what we can achieve in our current *now*.

We can choose to exercise personal process improvement strategies on any role that supports the pursuit of either physical or spiritual immortality. I believe that, especially in modern society, *most of these roles involve a relationship with another human being*. These roles may serve goals of major or minor importance to us. They may turn out to be a goal of major importance to others and, if achieved, *make us one of the major social process improvers of our time*. Or, they may be of no importance to anyone else at all. The most important thing is that these goals *hold meaning for us as individuals*.

We then execute a process improvement strategy and if we *perceive* that that strategy has improved the outcome of the process, we then subconsciously know that we, *as the executors of those processes,* have improved. From this we derive the personal renaissance experience that generates happiness in our lives.

Ultimately, when we die, our unique, *physical* identities end.

I believe we all possess a unique spiritual identity. We can discover this in ourselves once we recognize and defer to a level of consciousness well beyond our own. When this happens, we can better accept our flawed nature, and experience the peace that the act of self-forgiveness provides. We then, through *a kind of knowing* distinct from the kind we employ to understand our natural surroundings, are able to commune with this superior consciousness (the "*Transcendent Consciousness*"). This communion can carry us closer to the creative force that brought all of what is currently known (not really that much) and unknown (an unfathomable amount) into existence. I believe that this connection carries on after the end of our physical lives and allows our *now metaphysical selves* to exist solely in the realm of the Transcendent Consciousness. And, while we are still living on Earth, that connection also helps us to do our best to live according to the evolving set of standards that we, informed by that Transcendent Consciousness, set for ourselves.

Whether we are acting in the pursuit of physical or spiritual immortality, we, in essence, are purposefully continuing the process of human evolution. We do this on a personal level by our attempts to make improvements in as many of the dimensions of our being as feasible. We, in a very real sense, become artists creating successive iterations of self that bring us from states of varying degrees of chaos to greater order. This process pleases us and rewards us with feelings of fulfillment. Just as God, described in Genesis, was pleased with the results of his work after finishing his creation of the world with the creation of mankind ("...*it was very good.*"), so too can all of us be very pleased through our individual efforts at *self "re-creation"*.

www.ingramcontent.com/pod-product-compliance
Lightning Source LLC
LaVergne TN
LVHW040154080526
838202LV00042B/3160